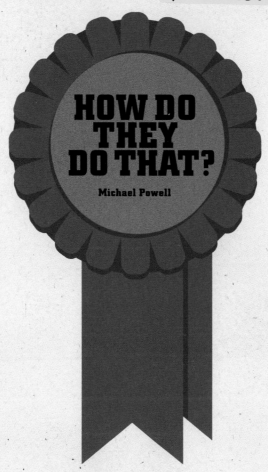

HOW DO THEY DO THAT?

Michael Powell

BARNES & NOBLE

NEW YORK

PUBLISHER'S NOTE

The people described in this book have neither contributed to this
book in any way, nor endorsed its content. The information contained in
this book is for entertainment purposes only.

Published exclusively for Barnes & Noble, Inc., by Gusto Company AS

Additional copyright information is available on p. 144.

© 2005 Gusto Company AS
Written by Michael Powell
Executive editor and original concept by James Tavendale
Designed by Allen Boe

ISBN 0-7607-7213-4

05 06 07 08 09 M 6 5 4 3 2 1

HOW DO THEY DO THAT?

Michael Powell

CONTENTS

INTRODUCTION

Genius is an elusive quality, easy to spot but almost impossible to describe. What was it that made Sir Edmund Hillary tower above his contemporaries? It wasn't his climbing ability. What makes Matt Groening one of the funniest guys on the planet? It isn't what he learned at school. What enabled Jean Driscoll to be such an outstanding athlete? It wasn't just her strength and fitness.

These virtuosos view the world, as well as their place in it, differently than the rest of us. Their achievements are no accident. Their talents, ignited by passion, glow white-hot when inflamed by dauntless conviction, tenacity, and years of self-sacrifice. Above all, they strive for simplicity, whether it's Bruce Lee honing his unique fighting style, Jane Goodall observing primate behavior, or Ansel Adams capturing the secrets of nature.

That's why we've added a neat feature that ties photograph to text and highlights some important traits. Each paragraph or group of paragraphs forms part of a checklist, and has a box next to it with a letter. If the box is checked, it corresponds to the letter on the photograph.

Here's Dan Marino throwing a football. The ball is labeled (a) and it corresponds to the paragraph, which describes how he grips the ball. There's a letter (c) pointing to his body, matching the paragraph which describes his stance. His throwing arm is labeled (d) and tallies with the section explaining how he winds up the throw. It's easier than a-b-c.

This book won't turn you into a genius but it will help you to understand how these remarkable superstars do what they do. The dedication that goes into being a top athlete, entertainer, scientist, inventor, politician, or writer is humbling and awe-inspiring. Knowing what makes them tick won't make their exploits seem any less profound. In fact, the more you read about these illustrious high-flyers, the more you will admire them and appreciate why they are truly legends in their fields.

THINK LIKE EINSTEIN

Born:	**March 14, 1879**
Birthplace:	**Ulm, Germany**
Died:	**April 18, 1955**

Developed the special theory of relativity, made important contributions to quantum field theory, and received a Nobel Prize in 1921 for his work on the photoelectric effect.

In 1905, Albert Einstein was a young patent clerk who, in his spare time, addressed the most fundamental problems in physics of his age. He published five groundbreaking papers which proved the existence of atoms, presented his special theory of relativity, and established quantum theory. But how did he do it? What was so special about his brain and his thinking processes that enabled him to revise fundamental notions of space and time, and to stand shoulder to shoulder with Isaac Newton in the pantheon of scientific geniuses?

IN HIS OWN WORDS

When he was sixteen, Einstein wrote a school essay in which he talked about his plans for the future and his perceived strengths which had made him aim for this path: "Above all it is my individual disposition for abstract and mathematical thought, my lack of imagination, and practical talent. My inclinations have also led me to this resolve. That is quite natural; one always likes to do things for which one has talent. And then there is a certain independence in the scientific profession which greatly pleases me."

Later he wrote, "I soon learned to scent out what was able to lead to fundamentals and to turn aside from everything else, from the multitude of things that clutter up the mind."

There are five important factors here which help to explain his genius: his capacity for abstract and mathematical thought; his lack of practical talent; his desire for independence; his ability to perceive fundamentals (and simplicity); and his incredible focus.

WAS HE A LATE DEVELOPER?

Many people have seized on Einstein's apparent failure at school as a sign that he may have had a learning disability, maybe Asperger's syndrome (a form of autism). He was certainly very unhappy in one of his schools, but this had more to do with its emphasis on rote learning and its petty authoritarianism than with his poor grades. Although he excelled at mathematics, he did not thrive at school in Munich; even at the age of nine he was described by his family and friends as quiet, contemplative, and slow to talk. It was only after he had left school and was working in a secure, well-paid job that he could devote all his energies to his passion.

WAS HIS BRAIN DIFFERENT?

After Einstein's death in 1955, Dr. Thomas Harvey, the pathologist who performed the postmortem, removed Einstein's brain and cut it into sections to see if any parts of it were abnormal. He found nothing unusual. However, Canadian scientists recently discovered that the region of the brain which deals with visual, spatial, and mathematical thinking was fifteen percent wider than other brains. His brain also lacked a small

groove (the parietal operculum) which may have allowed the neurons
to communicate more effectively. Professor Sandra Witelson, who led
the research, said, "Einstein's own description of his scientific thinking
was that words did not seem to play a role. Instead he saw more or
less clear images of a visual kind."

d ☒ MAKING CONNECTIONS

We have already seen that Einstein thought visually rather than in
terms of mathematics or words, but another important trait was his
ability to look at a problem from a different perspective. The physicist
Abraham Pais says that he was "better than anyone before or after
him" at inventing "invariance principles." In other words, he dared to
challenge beliefs about which things were constant and which could
change. Everyone else assumed that time and distance were fixed
and that the speed of light wasn't. Einstein showed that the opposite
was the case, and also that space was curved. He didn't invent the
concepts of energy, mass, or speed of light; he simply combined them
in a novel way.

e ☐ SENSE OF RESPONSIBILITY

Sir Martin Rees, British Astronomer Royal, points out a characteristic
of Einstein's thinking which most of us ignore: that he didn't say that
he was just a scientist "and that the use made of [his] work was up to
politicians. . . . We need the kind of perspective that Einstein himself
espoused—global, humanistic, and long term. If we choose wisely,
Einstein's legacy will resonate through this century and indeed far
beyond."

FIGHT LIKE BRUCE LEE

Born:	November 27, 1940
Birthplace:	San Francisco, California, USA
Died:	July 20, 1973

Widely considered to be the greatest martial arts movie actor/director of the twentieth century, and hailed by many as the epitome of mental and physical perfection.

This section does not seek to turn you into a martial arts expert. Instead, it attempts to convey some of the qualities and the philosophy which set Bruce Lee apart from other martial arts practitioners, and to show why he is still considered by many to be the best fighter who ever lived.

a ☐ TWO TURNING POINTS

Not surprisingly, his amazing fighting ability was created by the way in which he used and trained both mind and body. But there are at least two key events in his life which spurred him to be the best. The first was being beaten up by a street gang when he was thirteen. It was then that he started learning *Kung Fu*, studying under a master who actually encouraged his students to develop by getting into street fights. The second turning point was in 1965, when he was twenty-four and already arguably the best fighter in the world. He was teaching martial arts in his own small San Francisco fighting school to anyone, not just Chinese people. For this he was challenged to a no-holds barred fight by Wong Jack Man, a leading *Kung Fu* expert who felt, as did many in the Chinatown community, that Lee was betraying his race. Lee won

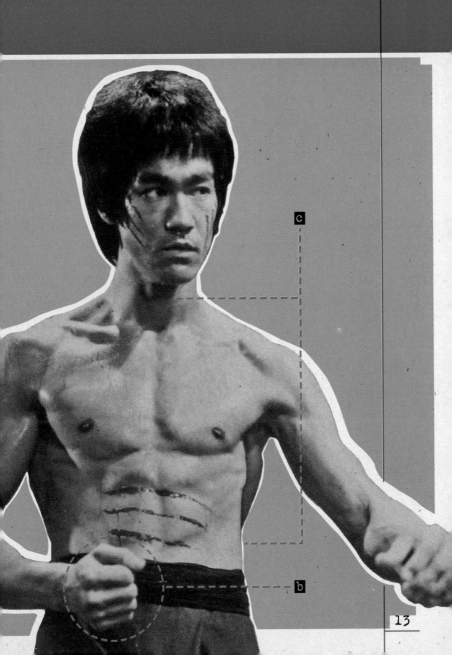

c

b

quickly and convincingly (the fight mainly consisted of Wong Jack Man running away from Lee), but he was alarmed at how much it took out of him. He felt that he should have dispatched his opponent much more effectively, so he began to focus upon cardiovascular training and perfecting *Jeet Kune Do*, his unique fighting technique.

b ☒ ## WHAT WAS HIS FIGHTING PHILOSOPHY?

Lee was a street fighter who distrusted technique for its own sake. He criticized the empty rituals, endless repetitions, and dogmatic instruction methods of institutionalized martial arts, which were hierarchical and taught blind obedience to the Master. Lee always explained why a move was effective before he taught it. He sought to strip away anything that was superfluous, always simplifying to reach the cleanest and most direct way to respond to an attack and disable an assailant. He taught his students to respond to an attack with spontaneity and individuality, rather than try to straightjacket them with technique: "Learn the principle, abide by the principle, and dissolve the principle." He brought martial arts, street fighting, and common sense together for the first time.

Jeet Kune Do means "The Way of the Intercepting Fist" and this aptly sums up his philosophy of intercepting and attacking at the same time. It went against conventional martial arts which taught that you should block an attack and then attack. Lee felt this was slower and less efficient since it involved two moves rather than one. He believed "the highest technique is to have no technique. My technique is a result of your [the attacker's] technique; my movement is a result of your movement."

Although his students included famous actors such as James Coburn and Steve McQueen, Bruce Lee was totally opposed to putting the teacher on a pedestal. "There is no mystery about my style. My movements are simple, direct, and non-classical. The extraordinary part of it lies in its simplicity."

c ☒ HOW DID HE TRAIN HIS BODY?

Bruce Lee's physique has been admired by athletes, movie-goers, and even bodybuilders for its lean, solid muscle definition. Bodybuilding tycoon Joe Weider called it "the most defined body I've ever seen." There is a famous anecdote about how the wife of the director of *Enter the Dragon* exclaimed on squeezing his arm muscles, "It's like feeling warm marble."

His body didn't just look good. It looked good because it had been trained to be functional, for speed and strength. Lee was only interested in strength and muscle that could be converted into power, and he actually reduced his muscle mass when he felt that it hampered his agility. He trained to get the maximum results with the minimum effort. While he may have trained his abdominal muscles tirelessly, he didn't spend hours in the gym—he was a consummate multi-tasker. He read everything he could find about training specific muscles and picked the most efficient methods; if a piece of training equipment didn't exist, he had it built. Ever practical, he trained his punches and kicks against hard targets such as focus gloves and body bags, rather than kicking into thin air.

Above all, he believed that in combat "spontaneity rules; rote performance of technique perishes." Put together his philosophy and physical training and the result (in Lee's own words) is "the art of expressing the human body."

DRIVE LIKE MICHAEL SCHUMACHER

Born: **January 3, 1969**

Birthplace: **Hürth-Hermülheim, Germany**

FIA Formula 1 World Champion in 1994, 1995, 2000, 2001, 2002, 2003, and 2004, and holds the record for the most Grand Prix triumphs ever.

Michael Schumacher is the highest paid athlete in the world. He has been the Formula 1 World Champion seven times, and earns an estimated $90 million per year. For the last six years he has dominated Formula 1 to such an extent that recently many sweeping rule changes have been made by the sport's governing body in an attempt to make the outcome less predictable. Nevertheless, if history is anything to go by, Schumacher's adaptability will allow him and his Ferrari team to stay at the top.

a ☐ WHERE DID SCHUMACHER START RACING?

His parents ran a small karting track just outside Cologne, Germany, so he got into karting when he was four years old and raced competitively in his teens. He got his big break in 1989 with Willi Weber's Formula 3 team. In 1991 he made his F1 debut as a replacement driver for Bertrand Gachot. He finished in seventh place, a staggering achievement for a rookie, and was immediately signed by sponsor Benetton. In 1994 and 1995, he won his first two championship titles.

b

WHAT MAKES HIM SO SPECIAL?

The extreme physical and mental stresses that motor racing places on a driver's body—G-forces, the high temperature in the cockpit, the need to make split-second tactical decisions—means that only those who have consummate physical fitness and stamina can expect to maintain their concentration for the duration of a race.

The stress, adrenaline, and physical exertion generated by a race means that drivers experience significantly elevated heart rates for an extended period of time. Michael Schumacher prepares for this off the track by doing hours of calisthenics and aerobic sports, such as running and soccer, on top of the hours of testing he does inside the car. Top F1 drivers are some of the fittest athletes in the world, and among his F1 peers, Schumacher's physical fitness is unrivalled.

Inside the car, one of his most important qualities is his ability to adapt quickly and make hundreds of instant decisions during a race. In 2003, he told London's *The Observer* newspaper: "Probably the biggest challenge you have as a racing driver, the biggest factor to affect the final result, is whether you adapt to this challenge, or not."

But pure talent isn't enough to keep him at the top of his sport. Schumacher is king not because he is the best driver (his peers agree that accolade should go to Giancarlo Fisichella), but because he is a "venture capitalist in a flame-retardant red jumpsuit." He also knows more about mechanics than most mechanics, and with his technical knowledge he could outsmart Bill Gates.

C ☐ **TEAM WORK**

In the 1990s, he transformed Ferrari and with it the whole sport of Formula 1, which is now a technology war, thanks largely to him and his team. Schumacher knew the importance of building a team and technologies around him that played to his strengths and driving style. He is Teutonic, rather than charismatic, but his leadership qualities come from his iron self-belief, his strategic excellence, and also his amazing talent for driving.

He has developed the sort of business skills that wouldn't be out of place in a blue-chip company. If he wasn't a racing driver, he'd have made even more money as one of the top CEOs in the world. He works hard, plays by the rules (gamesmanship aside), and outsmarts the competition.

COMPOSE A SONG
LIKE ELTON JOHN

Born: March 25, 1947

Name at birth: Reginald Kenneth Dwight

Birthplace: Pinner, Middlesex, UK

Singer, composer, and pianist. A child prodigy on the piano,
he won a scholarship to London's Royal Academy of Music when
he was eleven. He is one of the world's most versatile and
bestselling pop singers.

**Sir Elton John's flamboyant personality, his innate show-
manship, and his considerable musical talent have made
him one of pop music's most enduring icons. He is second
only to Elvis Presley in popularity, having produced consistent hits for more than thirty years.**

WRITTEN IN THE STARS

Much of John's compositional style is drawn from composers who he
admired. Among them are Peter Tchaikovsky and Jean Sibelius. Sibelius
was also heavily influenced by Tchaikovsky, which is especially apparent in his choral symphony, "Kullervo," and his "Symphony No. 1 in E
Minor." Sibelius sought to radically simplify the music's internal construc-
tion, as does John in most of his compositions.

Contemporary American artists influenced him as well. John grew up
listening to Elvis, Guy Mitchell, and Johnny Ray. "I think that as a pianist
I used to copy Little Richard and Jerry Lee Lewis and Fats Domino, and
then Ray Charles," John said in an interview. But when composing, there
was just one contemporary influence: "I copied Leon Russell," he said,
"and that was it."

d

b ☐

YOUR SONG

One of his first hits, "Your Song," is composed in binary form, with the verse repeating before the chorus. Binary form was often used to structure movements for sonatas written for keyboards. It was used during the Romantic period, when Tchaikovsky wrote, and in the simpler Modern period, when Sibelius composed.

The binary form, traditionally, is two halves, equal in length. The first half starts in one key and finishes in another; the second half begins in the key that ended the first half and finishes with the work's initial key—visually, A-B/B-A. Binary form is substantially different than the verse-chorus form common to most popular music.

c ☐

CAN YOU FEEL THE LOVE TONIGHT?

Many of his songs also follow a pattern of a slowly building crescendo that climaxes with a *tutti* finish. That's especially noticeable in "Don't Let the Sun Go Down on Me" and "Rocket Man." *Tutti*, Italian for *all*, refers to a concerto section in which the orchestra plays while the soloist is silent—and orchestration is another of the unique elements in Elton John's music. In the electric-guitar-laden 1970s, only John and Billy Joel reached prominence with a lead piano. John's compositions were written for the piano, then orchestrated by someone else, usually Paul Buckmaster.

"The biggest influence on me from a production standpoint and a song writing point of view was Brian Wilson," John said, ". . . Brian Wilson is a genius and always will be."

d ☒ ## DON'T SHOOT ME;
I'M ONLY THE PIANO PLAYER

Bernie Taupin wrote the lyrics for most of John's hits. "Without Bernie, there would be no Elton," John has said. They rarely worked together; Taupin would send the lyrics and John composed the music without changing a word. Both worked quickly, sometimes finishing a song with each of them putting in just half an hour. As John composed to Taupin's lyrics, he covered a spectrum of styles: blues, ballads, and musical parody. Yet the sad songs are often considered his best (after all, they say so much).

"I'm a melody person, so I can sit down and write a song, and I know it's going to sound really beautiful, and I know this is going to sound boastful, but something like 'Sorry Seems to be the Hardest Word' or 'Your Song,' I can write that sort of melody every day," John said. "I find it harder, because I'm a pianist, to write a good up-tempo song."

e ☐ ## I'M STILL STANDING

John intentionally reverted to his 1970s style by the late 1990s. But he also branched out, composing the Oscar-winning music for *The Lion King,* writing music for *Aida,* and then creating two new musicals, *Billy Elliot* and *Vampire Lestat.* For the musicals, John writes the songs in chronological order, basing them on the show's plot line and characters.

Ultimately, it's still Elton John. As he said when he returned to his 1970s style, "You can only be yourself."

PAINT LIKE PICASSO

Born:	October 25, 1881
Birthplace:	Málaga, Spain
Died:	April 8, 1973

One of the most influential artists of the twentieth century and a creator of Cubism.

Pablo Picasso mastered a plethora of styles and media: Realism, Neo-classicism, even lithography, sculpture, and ceramics. But the soul of his work, that for which he is most remembered, are his Cubist paintings, a style that took Impressionism a step further and launched a new approach to art in the twentieth century.

LOOKING AT LIFE DIFFERENTLY

Although the Impressionists were the first to move away from Realism by not painting subjects as they appeared to the eye, Picasso was the first to look in and around the subject. Traditional painters —even the Impressionists—depicted their subjects in two dimensions, creating the illusion of depth by adding shadows and perspective. But Picasso believed the subject should be represented as it was genuinely experienced in life—from many angles rather than a single point of view.

To paint like Picasso, one must represent the whole subject on canvas, be it a tree or a person. When we see a tree in a forest, we walk

a
d

b

around it, we touch it, we see it from all sides and angles. Similarly, when we see a person, we see more than their face with one expression—we see in that person a complexity of moods, thoughts, emotions, and actions, we see them move, hear them speak, and, if we know them well, we know their heart. Picasso believed that all of that—whether the tree or the person—should appear in a painting if it were to be a true representation of the subject.

"The goal I proposed myself in making Cubism?" he was quoted as saying in the 1932 publication, *Del Pomar, Con las Buscadores del Camino*. "To paint and nothing more. And to paint seeking a new expression, divested of useless realism, with a method linked only to my thought—without enslaving myself with objective reality. Neither the good nor the true; neither the useful nor the useless."

SUBJECTS IN PLANE VIEW

Picasso showed the many facets of his subjects by capturing each element of the subject on a different plane. Although his paintings were flat, Picasso took the individual planes—also called cubes, giving rise to the movement's name—and pieced them together to represent the whole of the subject. When painting people, he often placed a plane showing the subject's nose in profile on a face viewed from the front.

The technique is evidenced in such works as *Les Demoiselles d'Avignon, The Guitar Player,* and *Dora Maar.* Each of the perspectives—each cube—exists simultaneously.

c ☐ OTHER STYLES

While Picasso is most famous for originating the Cubist style—and
despite his derogatory comments about Realism—he produced many
realistic paintings during his prolific career. His earliest works, known
as his Blue Period, featured accomplished realistic depictions heavily
toned with shades of blue. Among his paintings from that time were
The Old Guitar Player, *Le Gourmet*, and *Blue Nude*. His brighter Rose
Period followed, also displaying his Realism skills but in a different
dominant hue.

Yet to paint like Picasso is not to be limited to Cubism or Realism; later
in his career he painted in the Surrealist and Neo-Classical styles.

d ☒ EYES OF A CHILD

Even the youngest may be able to paint like Picasso. The simple,
clean lines in works such as *La Ronde*, *Petit Fleurs*, *Rooster*, and *The
Camel* have a light, childlike quality. But that was something Picasso
strove to achieve. As he remarked when visiting an exhibition of
children's drawings: "When I was their age I could draw like Raphael,
but it took me a lifetime to learn to draw like them."

BE HONEST LIKE
ABRAHAM LINCOLN

Born: **February 12, 1809**

Birthplace: **Hodgenville, Kentucky, USA**

Died: **April 15, 1865**

Sixteenth President of the United States and leader of the country through the Civil War. Remembered for his eloquence and integrity, and widely held to be the greatest American of all time.

There were many who didn't agree with Abraham Lincoln's politics; he won his first presidential term by a narrow plurality. But just try to find a record of anyone who questioned his honesty or his character—supporters and opponents alike held great respect for the Illinois lawyer.

HONEST ABE

The story that likely gave rise to the "Honest Abe" moniker came from his time as a shop clerk in New Salem, Illinois, in 1831. Lincoln was twenty-two years old then, minding a store owned by a businessman named Denton Offutt. A Mrs. Duncan came into the shop one afternoon and purchased two dollars and six cents worth of goods. She took her change and carried her purchases home, about two miles away. After closing the store that evening and presumably counting out the cash, the young Lincoln realized he'd made a mistake—he had inadvertently short-changed (or overcharged) Mrs. Duncan.

Some would have pocketed the extra money from the register. Some would have gone home and let the books show a small overage. Others

e

f

would have given the customer the difference the next time she came into the store. But Lincoln never saw room for play in the honesty line.

After securing the shop for the night, Lincoln walked to Mrs. Duncan's house and handed her the six cents she was due.

b ☐

HONEST TO A TEA

The other story from Offutt's that led to Lincoln's reputation was that of a woman who came into the store for a half-pound of tea. Lincoln weighed it out, packaged it up, and collected the money, then closed the shop for the night. When he came to work the next morning, he noticed that the weights balancing the scale added up to only four ounces. Lincoln promptly weighed out another four ounces of tea, which he delivered to the woman with his apology, before opening for the day.

Lincoln's reputation for fairness and honesty was so widespread in New Salem that he became the town's choice to serve as umpire in sports and arbitrator in disputes.

c ☐

DOING THE RIGHT THING. AGAIN.

A year later Lincoln and a partner owned a general store in New Salem, but the enterprise failed—or, in Lincoln's words, "winked out." A short while later Lincoln's partner died, but the twenty-three-year-old promised to repay the entire sum. He was good to his word, even though it took him more than fifteen years.

Lincoln again demonstrated that a genuinely honest person isn't only honest when it's convenient. He's honest regardless of personal cost.

d ☐ AN ETHICAL LAWYER

While Lincoln was practicing law, he often encouraged clients to avoid the expense of litigation and to settle matters out of court. It was contrary to his own financial interests, but beneficial to his clients. On one occasion, Lincoln and his law partner prevented a con-artist from taking a piece of land from a young, mentally-ill woman. When it came time to divide the fee, Lincoln insisted that at least half be returned to the client. "The money comes out of the pocket of a poor, demented girl, and I would rather starve than swindle her in this manner," he said.

e ☒ IN HIS OWN WORDS

"Let no young man choosing the law for a calling for a moment yield to the popular belief—resolve to be honest at all events; and if in your own judgment you cannot be an honest lawyer, resolve to be honest without being a lawyer."—*Notes for a Law Lecture*, July 1, 1850.

f ☒ HONESTY AND DIPLOMACY

During his presidency, his honesty was the cornerstone of his leadership and diplomacy. His trustworthiness enabled him to gain the cooperation of competing groups so that he could get them to work together toward a common goal. It was this that enabled him to mobilize and inspire the North to victory against the Confederacy and ultimately kept the Union intact.

HANG LIKE MICHAEL JORDAN

Born: **February 17, 1963**

Birthplace: **Brooklyn, New York, USA**

> The greatest player in the history of basketball with an NBA record career scoring average of 32.3. He was the first USA team athlete to license his own name and first retired at age thirty in 1993 saying, "I don't have anything else to prove."

So you want to hang like Mike? To dribble full court, elevate behind the free-throw line, and still have to duck your head to miss the rim, swing the ball over, and stuff it with both hands? WHAAAAMM!! Ladies and gentlemen, the laws of physics just left the building.

Okay, time to wake up and listen good if you want to know how your Royal Airness stops time. It seems like he just comes down to earth when he's—*reverse jam, windmill, double-pump, rock-the-cradle, no-look dunk*—finished whatever he wants to do up there.

SPEED, STAMINA, POWER

First off, he's one of the fittest athletes in the world. He can play basketball for long periods of time without needing to rest; this means he has awesome speed on tap when he needs it. Speed takes power, and he has a high proportion of fast-twitch muscle fibers (the kind you need for explosive power).

VERTICAL AND HORIZONTAL MOTION

But how much speed and power does it take to keep a two-hundred-pound NBA legend off the ground for one second (seems longer, doesn't it?)? Let's examine the physics and you'll see that you've got to be almost superhuman to grab that much air.

There are two components to his jump: vertical and horizontal motion. But it's only his vertical motion (or how much power he converts into vertical speed) that determines the hang time. It doesn't matter how far he jumps horizontally; it will have no bearing on how long he stays airborne.

The vertical height is related to the initial upward speed. The laws of physics mean that he's got to jump four feet vertically for a hang time of one second, and to do that he needs a vertical speed of sixteen feet per second at take-off. This means that the very best jumpers, who rarely exceed a vertical leap of four feet, never spend more than one second in the air—it just seems that way. To reach a hang time of two seconds, Michael would have to rise vertically sixteen feet!

C ☐

JUST AN ILLUSION

So how does he make it look so much longer? Well my friend, that's the Jordan magic, showmanship, whatever you want to call it. Sure, he pumps his arms, but that doesn't help, because once you're airborne, unless you've got feathers, you can't generate more vertical lift. All the power is created by his legs pushing against the ground. Biomedical scientists have calculated that he produces a force of about three times his body weight on take-off—that's about six hundred pounds.

Once he has launched he travels in a perfect curve, but as soon as his feet leave the ground his body begins to lose vertical speed at a rate of thirty-two feet per second (about twenty-two mph). He continues to rise until at the tip of the curve his vertical speed is zero—that's the moment when he appears to hang. He will continue to move horizontally at a steady rate while showing very little up or down motion near the peak of the jump. It is this effect that creates the illusion of hanging in the air.

JUMP LIKE JACKIE JOYNER-KERSEE

Born: March 3, 1962

Birthplace: East St. Louis, Illinois, USA

The greatest heptathlete in the history of the sport. She has won three Olympic gold medals, a silver, and a bronze. She holds the women's world record for long jump at twenty-three-feet nine-inches. She was also the first woman to get more than 7,000 points in the heptathlon; her 1988 world record of 7,291 still stands today.

Unless you were born with her incredible physique, chances are that reading this section isn't going to make you jump as far as her, but these tips may well increase your length considerably. There are three main long-jump techniques: the Stride Jump, Hitch Kick, and the Hang style. There are four parts of the event: run-up, take-off, flight, and landing.

a ☐ RUN-UP

Long jumpers are usually great sprinters, because the higher the speed that they can reach on the run-up, the longer they travel in the air. But they need to balance their speed with their strength and technique. Sometimes it may be necessary to run slightly slower to achieve optimum technique before planting the leading foot on the take-off board powerfully and accurately.

Most athletes run from a standing start, which is the easiest way to ensure that the run-up distance is accurate. Athletes measure their run-up by placing their non-take-off foot on the take-off board and then sprinting backward a fixed number of steps (*e.g.*, twenty-one) and putting a marker on the place where the twenty-first step falls. Then they make a few practice jumps and move the marker back or forward depending on where they are taking off.

b ☒ TAKE-OFF

Just before take-off, the athlete instinctively changes body position in preparation, and this means that the hips sink and then rise again, so that the second-to-last stride is longer than the others and the last stride is the shortest (up to ten inches shorter than normal). This is a natural consequence of the body preparing for take-off, but there should be minimal loss of speed.

The take-off board should be struck with the heel first, so that the body weight rolls through the foot onto the ball and finally onto the toes. In this way, maximum vertical lift can be achieved.

c ☐ STRIDE JUMP

This is the technique most beginners choose, and it involves maintaining the take-off position for as long as possible in the air until the legs have to be straightened for the landing.

d ☐ HITCH KICK METHOD

After take-off, the free leg is straightened and the leading leg is flexed at the thigh in a stride position. Then the leading leg is rotated backward and straightened and the jumper appears for a moment to be running in mid-air. This corrects the forward rotation, so that the athlete's upper

body stays upright and so the body can stay in the air longer. At the end of the jump both legs come forward and are flexed for the landing. The arms rotate forward and back to assist in the landing.

HANG STYLE

On take-off the leading leg is driven upward, while the other leg drops down to the vertical and is then joined by the take-off leg. Both legs are then bent at the knees as the straight arms come back, over the head, and forward until just before landing. The body is almost in a pike position, only the arms by now are hanging down vertically, having completed a full circle of motion. When the arms are above the head it looks like the athlete is hanging in the air.

LANDING

The aim of the landing is to get the heels as far away from the take-off point as possible. Once the athlete lands in the sandpit, the center of gravity needs to be forward so that the upper body falls forward. The jump is measured from the mark in the sand that is the furthest back; falling backward loses valuable distance.

ESCAPE LIKE HARRY HOUDINI

Born:	March 24, 1874
Name at Birth:	Erik Weisz
Birthplace:	Budapest, Hungary
Died:	October 31, 1926

An acrobat, illusionist, hypnotist, and puppeteer who achieved worldwide fame and fortune for his daring escapes from chains, ropes, and handcuffs.

In the spring of 1899, twenty-five-year-old Harry Houdini was struggling for recognition and was ready to quit show business for good. Then, in a beer hall in St. Paul, Minnesota, his act caught the attention of vaudeville impresario Martin Beck, who Houdini admitted "changed my whole Life's journey."

HANDCUFF KING

It was Houdini's ability to escape from handcuffs which so intrigued Beck and gave the mysteriarch early fame as the "Handcuff King." He wasn't the first performer to use it in his act, but he was the first to offer an open challenge to anyone and any lock; during his career he took handcuff escapology to an unprecedented level.

He developed this unusual talent while serving as an apprentice locksmith. In an autobiographical article, Houdini explained this career-changing event.

"One day whilst working as an apprentice in a locksmith's close by the police station, one of the young bloods of the town was arrested for some trivial offense. He tried to open his handcuffs with some keys he had on his person, and in the attempt broke off one of the keys in the lock . . . after breaking half-a-dozen saw-blades, the thought struck me to attempt to pick the lock. I succeeded in doing it, and the very manner in which I then picked the lock of the handcuff contained the basic principle which I employed in opening handcuffs all over the world. Not with a duplicate key, which seems to have been the only way others had of duplicating my performance."

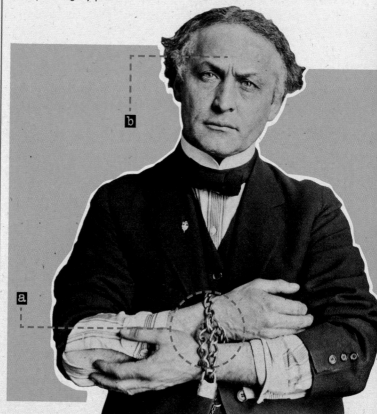

☒ LOCKED IN HIS MEMORY

He collected and studied locks throughout his life, and his acute visual memory enabled him to remember individual mechanisms and how to open them. He also used physical skill, trickery, and unprecedented showmanship. However, when he died he took with him many handcuff secrets that are still unknown today.

In 1910 he published *Handcuff Secrets*, to discourage the many imitators who were copying his act. Houdini wrote that "you can open the majority of the old-time cuffs with a shoestring. By simply making a loop in the string, you can lasso the end of the screw in the lock and yank the bolt back, and so open the cuff in as clean a manner as if opened with the original key."

☐ COGITATION OR DISLOCATION?

Often he had a key hidden about his person, or smuggled into his jail cell, but he also designed sets of picks which allowed him to reach keyholes not normally accessible while restrained. Often he manipulated the keys with his teeth. Some locks were easier than others; certain models simply opened when knocked in the right place. When several cuffs were used, he would ensure that the most difficult ones were placed on his flexed forearms, which would later be slipped over the other cuffs when he relaxed. He is also thought to have been able to dislocate several of his fingers. And of course, he wasn't averse to using trick cuffs which could be opened easily by slipping a fake rivet.

But it didn't end there; what began with handcuffs ended in Houdini's imprisonment in leg irons, milk cans, giant footballs, and just about anything else the world could dream up.

THROW A TOUCHDOWN PASS LIKE DAN MARINO

Born: September 15, 1961

Birthplace: Pittsburgh, Pennsylvania, USA

Statistically the greatest quarterback in the history of the NFL. When he retired in March 2000 after playing seventeen seasons, he was the all-time leader in touchdown passes (420), yardage (61,361), completions (4,967), and attempts (8,358).

Dan Marino started breaking records in his rookie season. He's not the world's best runner, but he doesn't need to be when he can throw a football over three hundred feet. Ronnie Lott, a Hall of Fame defensive back, sums up his awesome ability: "All the great ones see the game so quickly that when everybody else is running around like a chicken with his head cut off, they know exactly where they want to go with the ball. It's like they see everything in slow motion."

He is six-feet four-inches tall with a powerful right arm and he's a genius when it comes to throwing the ball where he knows one of his teammates will be seconds later. But there is a lot of technique involved in making the throw. And it takes years of practice to throw perfect passes: "When I was ten," admits Marino, "I entered the NFL Gatorade Punt, Pass, and Kick contest. I came in forty-eighth place. My passing stunk!! I went right home, painted a target on my tree and started throwing. And throwing. And throwing. And throwing . . ."

a

c

d

43

a ☒   GRIP

Marino grips toward the back of the ball and interlaces some of his fingers with the laces. The rest point toward the nose of the ball. He has large hands, so for him this is easy.

b ☐   PROTECTING THE BALL

He keeps the ball close to his chest, under his chin, with both hands until he has picked his target and is ready to throw.

c ☒   STANCE

He spreads his legs shoulder-width apart and turns his body so that his left shoulder faces the direction he wants the ball to go. Top quarterbacks like Marino need to be able to size up the passing opportunities in a split second, otherwise they get smoked by the opposition's defensive line.

d ☒   WINDING UP THE THROW

Marino pulls his right arm back and bends his elbow, keeping it higher than his shoulder for a short throw, or dipping his shoulder for a longer one. His weight is on his back (right) foot.

e ☐   THE THROW

He snaps his throwing arm forward, elbow first, followed by a whipping forearm, and then follows through with his shoulders and hips square up to the target as he transfers his weight to his left foot. This twisting of hips and the push from the back leg create his power. The speed comes from how quickly the throw is executed, and by making the ball spin in a tight spiral (just as the spiraling inside of a gun barrel makes the bullet spin and go faster).

f □ SPIRAL

He adds spin to the ball by pulling his arm in slightly to the left, releasing the ball pinkie first, followed by his fingers and thumb last, as he snaps his wrist and fingers down. After the ball leaves his hands, he follows through with his fingers, and his thumb ends up pointing downward. This is why breaking a thumb on the helmet of a three-hundred-and-fifty-pound lineman is an occupational hazard for quarterbacks.

g □ PLAY LIKE A ROOKIE

Marino played like a seasoned pro during his rookie year, but he maintained his rookie hunger for the game during his whole career, never losing the edge, never having to fake the feeling that the game was everything. Besides being motivated by his love of the game, Marino admits, "Silencing your critics is an awesome feeling."

HIT A HOME RUN LIKE BABE RUTH

Born: February 6, 1895

Name at Birth: George Herman Ruth

Birthplace: Baltimore, Maryland, USA

Died: August 16, 1948

Arguably the best baseball player of all time, he dominated the sport in a career that spanned three decades, and he was the first player to hit sixty home runs in a season. His record .690 lifetime slugging percentage may never be beaten.

Yankees teammate Lefty Gomez heaped on the praise: "No one hit home runs the way Babe did. They were something special. They were like homing pigeons. The ball would leave the bat, pause briefly, suddenly gain its bearings then take off for the stands." He changed the science of the game, which until that point had been much more tactical, exemplified by the likes of master tactician Ty Cobb—players hitting "small ball" and stealing bases to earn single runs. The Sultan of Swat didn't need such refinements—he just belted the ball over the bleachers. It is easy to forget that before Babe Ruth, home runs were freak occurrences.

His most famous homer must surely be in the 1932 World Series against the Chicago Cubs. The Great Bambino had two strikes and before the third pitch, he pointed to centerfield. He then proceeded to slug the ball out of Wrigley Field in that precise spot. The shot went down in baseball legend as the longest home run of that time.

Sorry folks: nobody can hit a home run like Babe Ruth, but there are ways to improve your speed and power.

a ☒ ## GRIPPING THE BAT

Hold the bat the same way you would hold an ax. If you are right-handed, place your left hand near the end of the bat and your right hand just above, lining up your knuckles. (If you bat left, like Ruth, reverse the placement of your hands.) The bat should be gripped tightly in the middle of the fingers, not in the palm of the hand.

Using a heavy bat will only make the ball travel further if you have the strength to use it properly. If it hampers your speed, then use a lighter bat, although some people recommend training with a heavier bat to build strength, then using a lighter bat in a game to feel much faster.

b ☐ ## STANCE

A comfortable and relaxed stance is a personal preference, but you should have your knees slightly bent and your legs should be spread wide enough (but not too wide) to give you good balance and support. A little wider than shoulder width is the norm.

c ☐ ## RAISE THE BAT

Hold the bat near the top of the strike zone, with your hands just below shoulder height. Arms should be slightly bent, not extended.

d ☒ ## STEP IN

Step toward the pitch as the ball leaves the pitcher's hand and keep your eye on the ball until you hit it. The power is generated by transferring body weight from the back to the forward foot as you pivot on your back foot and rotate your body into the swing.

☒ SWING

During the swing, the elbows should be kept close to the body so that the bat sweeps around in a tight circle through the strike zone. The faster the swing, the more energy is transferred to the ball, although the swing needs to be smooth and even.

☒ FOLLOW THROUGH

Bring the bat through until it finishes between your shoulder blades.

☐ DEVELOP STRENGTH AND SPEED

The best way to do this is to swing a bat—this builds arm strength and works on your hand grip while improving your swing technique. Weight train to build strength; do gripping exercises (including rollups and rolldowns) to improve your grip and to increase wrist and finger strength.

Remember, when you hit the ball you just have to explode. That's the bit that comes from within and can't be taught. It comes from the force of a person's personality, aggression, and desire to show the rest of the world that they're the best hitter in the history of the game.

WRITE A BESTSELLER LIKE STEPHEN KING

Born:	September 21, 1947
Birthplace:	Portland, Maine, USA

One of the most successful authors in the world, best-known for his horror stories including *Carrie* and *The Shining*.

Just how successful is Stephen King? One estimate puts his net worth at more than $200 million, with more than 100 million copies of his books having been sold.

HAVE SOME TALENT

A bit of talent helps. Critical essays on King's work go into great detail about his characters, his tone, and his plot structure. His pattern is to set a tone and build it throughout the novel, taking the apparently mundane and adding a layer of creepiness page by page until the ordinary—a car, a dog, a hotel, a fan—has become extraordinary. His characters are ordinary people thrown into extraordinary situations, but they are the crux of his writing style. King abhors plot outlines. Instead, he envisions his characters, puts them in a situation, and allows them to play it out.

Defining talent is akin to answering the meaning of life question. Yet King defines it in highly practical terms: "People who are published steadily and are paid for what they are writing may be either saints or trollops, but they are clearly reaching a great many someones who want

a

d

e

what they have. Ergo, they are communicating. Ergo, they are talented. The biggest part of writing successfully is being talented, and in the context of marketing, the only bad writer is one who doesn't get paid."

b ☐

PRACTICAL METHODS

King sold a few stories to horror magazines while he was in high school, but his break came at age twenty-seven when *Carrie* was published. Persistence paid off for King. He didn't give up after a few rejection slips and doesn't recommend giving up after dozens. But after thousands? He says: "My friend, after six thousand pinks, it's time you tried painting or computer programming."

He knows the markets, submitting work to publications most likely to buy it. "Only a dimwit would send a story about giant vampire bats surrounding a high school to *McCall's*," King says. And he follows the rules. If a submissions editor wants it double-spaced, he sends it that way. If they want a self-addressed, stamped envelope included, he sends that, too.

c ☐

GETTING INTO THE ZONE

Athletes often talk about getting into "the zone," but writers do it too—especially King. When he writes, he only writes. He doesn't look up synonyms in a thesaurus or spellings in a dictionary because those details can be corrected later, and the interruption breaks the writing flow. "When you sit down to write, write," he says. "Don't do anything else except go to the bathroom, and only do that if it absolutely cannot be put off."

☒ WRITING TO ENTERTAIN

King is an outspoken proponent of writing to entertain readers. That doesn't mean entertaining fiction and so-called serious fiction are mutually exclusive. King weaves in occasional social commentary and observations on the human condition, but he doesn't shout his views through a megaphone; he whispers them in a purely entertaining tale.

☒ EDITING AND EDITING THE EDITING

"If you haven't marked up your manuscript a lot, you did a lazy job," King says. "Only God gets things right the first time." Many of those marks are deletions. On a first draft, King often cuts about ten percent of the work just by getting rid of extraneous words.

☐ CRITICISM

King listens carefully to what eight or ten people have to say. If they all agree that a particular something isn't quite right, he cuts it or changes it. If they each point to something different, he ignores them all. And King is perhaps his most strident critic, unafraid to scrap a project and start over.

As he says, "When it comes to people, mercy killing is against the law. When it comes to fiction, it is the law."

BE A RENAISSANCE MAN LIKE LEONARDO DA VINCI

Born:	**April 15, 1452**
Birthplace:	**Anchiano, Republic of Florence** (now in Italy)
Died:	**May 2, 1519**

Painter, sculptor, architect, engineer, and the embodiment of the Renaissance spirit for knowledge and scientific enquiry. His *Mona Lisa* is one of the most famous paintings in the world.

Da Vinci was raised by his father who recognized early his artistic talent and sent him to apprentice with Andrea del Verrochio in Florence at age fourteen. Perhaps because of his widely varied interest and relentless pursuit of knowledge, da Vinci finished only a handful of paintings in his sixty-seven years.

As seems to be the case with many geniuses, da Vinci had his quirks. He wrote his personal notes in reverse, making them easily read by others only if held to a mirror. And when he worked, whether on a sculpture, painting, invention, or the dissection of a cadaver, he preferred a small, tidy studio.

ARTIST

Da Vinci painted as though the subject was viewed through a window, and he was fascinated by light. Although he was not the first to dabble in Realism, he vastly advanced the style by obsessively observing nature and recording what he saw in sketches and notes. His scientific approach led him to create depth in his work not only by using rigid techniques of perspective, but also by duplicating the appearance and color changes of objects in the distance. Among his revelations was that the farther away an object was, the more it takes on the characteristics of the atmosphere. If an object in a painting was close to the observer, he used its actual colors. The farther in the distance an object was, the more blue he used.

Da Vinci preferred to paint when the sky was overcast because the diffused light produced no distortions from shadows. If clouds were unavailable, he opted for a north window because the light didn't change as the day progressed.

To critique his work, da Vinci took frequent breaks, which gave him an opportunity to clear his mind and observe the painting at a glance. The technique tends to reveal any major problems in the work. He was also fond of holding the painting in front of a mirror.

He wrote: "When you paint look at your work in a mirror; when you see it reversed, it will appear to you like some other painter's work and you will be a better judge of its faults."

b ☐

INVENTOR

Da Vinci's habit of studying the world and making sketches and notes equally influenced his work as an engineer, inventor, and architect. He observed existing machines, noted how their gears and levers interacted, and created improvements and new machines based on the fundamental components. That analysis led to plans for a helicopter and a submarine. He studied how birds flew and fish swam, then drew plans for flying machines and underwater breathing hoods and webbed gloves.

c ☒

SCIENTIST

Driven by curiosity and a desire for knowledge, da Vinci was fascinated not just by the physical sciences, but also by astronomy. There was neither refrigeration nor formaldehyde in da Vinci's time, but he routinely obtained and dissected the bodies of deceased prisoners, studying the relationships between muscles, nerves, organs, and bones. As was his practice in the visual arts and engineering, da Vinci observed, studied, sketched, and took notes of every detail. Looking heavenward, his careful observations allowed him to diagram and calculate the distances between the earth, moon, and sun.

SERVE LIKE ANDY RODDICK

Born:	**August 30, 1982**
Birthplace:	**Omaha, Nebraska, USA**

Not only is he the youngest American in the history of the Association of Tennis Professionals (ATP) to end the tennis season ranked No. 1, he is also the fastest server in the game, and holds the world record for the massive 155-mph serve which he produced during the 2004 Davis Cup semi-final.

The key to his fast serve is that he generates a large amount of power in his body, then transfers it into racket speed, and then to the ball. It's no wonder some of his service games last all of twenty seconds.

THE THROW

Roddick throws the ball up and forward. The further away from his body the ball is thrown, the further he has to move his body weight forward to hit it, and the more power this generates. He could literally throw and serve the ball with his eyes closed because he has developed the balance and the timing to aim the ball precisely.

As he lifts his left arm into the throw, he brings his left knee forward, which begins to shift his body weight forward, and most importantly he keeps his knees bent, in preparation for driving them up.

b [X]

THE GRIP

Roddick grips the racket in a "chopper grip," so called because it is the same way that a person would hold an ax. Notice how close to the end of the grip the hand is. This allows for greater leverage and therefore more acceleration of the racket head. The V of the thumb and index finger are slightly left of the top of the grip.

c [ ]

THE DRIVE

When the ball has reached the top of its throw, Roddick drives forward and up with his legs. This generates a huge amount of power, and enables him to hit the ball at a higher point for greater power.

d [ ]

THE SWING

Many bad players lead with their racket. Roddick leads with his body so that his hand and the racket have to generate even more speed in order to compensate and reach the ball. This increases acceleration and maximizes the force with which he hits the ball because, as the laws of physics state, force equals mass times acceleration.

e [ ]

THE HIT

On impact, Roddick ensures that the face of the racket is square on to the ball, by turning his hand and forearm out just before he hits the ball.

f [ ]

COMING IN TO THE NET

Sometimes he will allow the forward motion and impetus generated by the serve to carry him forward to the net, where he will be in a strong position to volley the return for a winning shot—assuming, of course, that his blistering speed or acing accuracy hasn't already won the point.

g X BABOLAT TECHNOLOGY

Even the best server in the game needs the best technology in his
hand, and his super-powered Babolat™ racket with interactive strings
is probably the most powerful racket on tour, allowing him to deprive
his opponents any play on the ball. He's also got built-in technology
of his own—he's six-feet three-inches tall, strong, and flexible, and
his real killer weapon is one of the hottest limbs in sporting history:
what's known in sporting circles as "one helluva live arm."

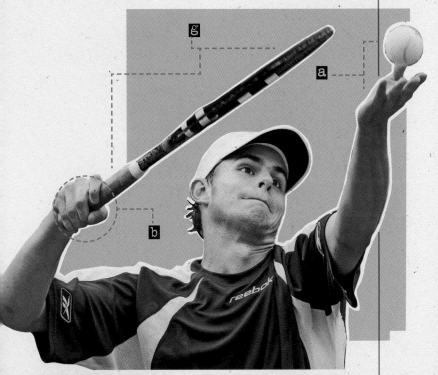

PUTT LIKE
BEN CRENSHAW

Born: **January 11, 1952**

Birthplace: **Austin, Texas, USA**

A major force in professional golf during the 1980s and 1990s, winning ten times on the PGA Tour, including the U.S. Masters in 1984 and 1995.

In the 1990s, Ben Crenshaw was involved in two of the most memorable moments in golfing history. The first occurred in 1995, when he took part in the U.S. Masters after the death of his mentor and legendary teacher, Harvey Penick. Crenshaw was one of the pallbearers at his funeral the day before the tournament began. Four days later he was Masters champion and collapsed in tears in his caddy's arms. The second piece of history occurred in 1999 when Crenshaw captained his trailing team to the largest Ryder Cup comeback ever. Golfer Willie Park famously said that "a man who can putt is a match for anyone." Crenshaw was one of the best in the game and he perfected the art of what he called "the dying putt."

GREEN AND SIMPLE

He has always kept his putting style simple. Crenshaw focuses on how fast he wants the ball to travel, then he allows a margin to the left or right of the hole, depending on the lie of the green. If it goes in the hole he considers it a bonus.

Instead of thinking about holing the ball, he tries to get it as close to the hole as possible. By taking the focus off the hole he can stay loose and focus on what he considers the most important factor: pace. He aims to get the speed right and the rest falls into place: "The ball which arrives at the hole with the proper speed has an infinitely greater chance of falling in the hole from any entrance. Harvey Penick taught me the value of this method at an early age. This is what he meant by 'giving luck a chance.'"

STANCE

He addresses the ball by leaning over it slightly with his hands just ahead of it, and then pivots from the shoulders to execute a slow and even stroke that appears effortless. Also, "it's important to think of the back swing and swing through the ball."

PERSONAL TOUCH

Like all greats in their chosen field, he has the humility, flexibility, and good sense to realize that there is no single way to putt a ball. He acknowledges, "There is really no right or wrong way to stand or set up. If you follow the sport, you know there have been many successful putters with radically different methods." But he does believe in some elements which are common to all good putters.

1 ☐ RELAXATION

Crenshaw believes that "consistent putts stem from consistent, solid strikes on the middle of the clubface. A solid hit is something you can usually hear and feel. So don't change your stroke too often, just try to meet the ball solidly."

2 ☒ KEEP YOUR HEAD DOWN

He is the first to admit that some of his worst putts have been because he has been too eager to see where the ball went. He recommends keeping your head down and curbing any temptation to see how good the shot was.

3 ☒ "LITTLE BEN"

This is the name of his putter which his father bought for him for just $20 when Ben was a child. He has used it ever since. He has filed the chrome and broken the shaft, and it has been stolen twice. His father explained: "It was just a putter in Harvey Penick's shop. Ben felt it and waggled it around for a while. 'Dad, I'd like to have it,' he said, so I bought it for him. That club's been the best provider in the family."

MAKE FRIENDS LIKE DALE CARNEGIE

Born:	**November 24, 1888**
Birthplace:	**Maryville, Missouri, USA**
Died:	**November 1, 1955**

Lecturer, bestselling author, salesman, and an expert in the psychology of success.

Dale Carnegie wasn't just about making friends—he put equal emphasis on getting them moved over to his point of view. But it went all the way around—the first and most important step for Carnegie was to get people to like him.

THE BASICS

Carnegie handed out praise the way an usher hands out programs at church. He never held back a kind word, distributing plenty of good words for all. But it was genuine—Carnegie believed in honest and sincere appreciation.

The second element of Carnegie's strategy was never to complain, condemn, or criticize. No one likes a whiner and no one wants to hear that they're wrong or bad.

Of course, Carnegie also wanted to influence people. The third element of his approach was to instill in people an eager want.

b

c

65

MAKING PEOPLE LIKE YOU

According to Carnegie, there were six components:

1. Be genuinely interested in other people. Real interest is a great form of flattery; disinterest communicates that the other person is boring at best, without value at worst.

2. Smile. It's hard to dislike a happy person.

3. Remember a person's name. After all, a person's own name is the sweetest and most important sound in any language.

4. Listen. Carnegie was a great listener and encouraged people to talk about themselves. We all want to believe someone finds us interesting.

5. Speak in terms of the other person's interests. (This expands on the first and fourth steps.)

6. Make the other person feel important and do so with sincerity. We are egocentric, Carnegie knew, and making other people the center of the universe—even if only during a brief encounter—makes them feel good. And it makes them like you.

GET THEM TO SEE IT YOUR WAY

Carnegie's approach to influence was much like his approach to making friends: Build egos, don't crush them. He consistently showed respect for others' opinions and never said, "You're wrong." If he was wrong, he would admit it readily and emphatically. If he wanted to persuade someone that an idea was good, he found a way to let them feel as if it were their idea. And he let them talk. A lot.

Carnegie thought that the only way to win an argument was to avoid it. He would get people to start agreeing with him on trivial points and keep them saying "yes" until it seemed they agreed on everything. As the conversation progressed, the importance of the agreement grew; by the time he got to the point he really wanted to make, it was easiest for the other person to just keep agreeing.

There is always another point of view, and when someone didn't share his, Carnegie made a bona fide effort to put himself in the other person's shoes and see what that person saw. It allowed him to express honest sympathy for the other person's view. That, of course, made the person feel validated and important.

He began every conversation in a friendly manner and when he hoped to persuade someone, he concluded by appealing to a nobler cause—then threw down a challenge: "Mr. Smith, I know you're the kind of man who wants his family to be safe and secure. You're not the sort that's going to risk their well being by failing to provide for them with a sound life insurance policy, are you?"

CENTER OF THE UNIVERSE

In short, Carnegie won friends (and customers) by making each of them feel like the most interesting, important person in the world—and it's awfully hard to dislike someone who makes you feel that way.

SKATE LIKE BONNIE BLAIR

Born: **March 18, 1964**

Birthplace: **Cornwall, New York, USA**

Speed skater and the most successful female Olympian.
She won five Olympic gold medals and one bronze.

When Bonnie Blair broke her own world record in the 500-meter speed skating event in 1994, she finished the course in 38.99 seconds. Even starting at a standstill, this meant an average speed of 28.7 miles per hour. She also set the American record in the 1000-meter event, where, on her thirty-first birthday, she again averaged 28.7 miles per hour. She did it with a combination of form and strength.

HER LEGS

Although Blair, at five-feet four-inches tall, is more petite than most speed skaters, she has exceptional strength in her quadriceps. With each stride, Blair extends her pushing leg almost straight out to the side, giving the width of her blade maximum contact time with the ice. While the bulk of the thrust comes from the thigh, Blair also rotates her ankle at the end of the stroke, giving the ice a sort of final flick—and that gets her an extra fraction of a second of contact.

HER FEET

When Blair finishes the propulsion stroke, she quickly pulls that foot back next to the other. Part of her success comes from the rapidity

f

e

a

b

d

with which she can shift her weight to the other foot and immediately begin another stroke with the opposite leg. Although short-distance speed skaters use a flat or nearly flat skate blade, Blair still glides on the outside edge of the blade, then rolls her foot to push with the inside edge, minimizing resistance and maximizing power.

HER WEIGHT

Blair's posture on the track helps force her weight to her heels, unlike running, where the weight is on the ball of the foot. By having her weight on her heels, Blair is able to extend her leg to the side; if she leaned forward and forced her weight to the ball, the skate would move almost straight back in a running motion, providing little thrust.

TURNS

Blair uses a crossover step to maneuver turns without interrupting propulsion, just as hockey players and figure skaters do. But Blair is pushing against the ice throughout the crossover rather than letting one skate glide. As her right leg crosses over the left, her left skate's outer edge grips the ice; she pulls with that leg, then shifts her weight to push off with the inside edge of her right skate. The combination gives her continuous power throughout the turn.

Look at photos or videos of Bonnie Blair during a race and you'll see that Blair's body isn't twisted at the turns—she keeps her body in a vertical line with her shoulders remaining perpendicular. As she leans into the turn, she turns her hips slightly in the direction of the curve, allowing her to keep her balance—and momentum.

☒ KEEPING LOW

You'll also notice in those images that she is bent so far over that her knees nearly touch her chest. By bending deeply at the waist, Blair is able to maintain her balance even though there's nearly a ninety-degree angle between her calf and thigh. The deep knee bend allows for greater extension of her leg when she pushes to the side and, correspondingly, more power.

☒ THE ARM SWING

Blair specialized in sprints rather than long-distance races, so endurance was less of an issue than a quick burst of power. Part of Blair's power comes from the force she generates with her arms, swinging the right arm over the left knee and vice versa. Her quick, striking motion allows her to maintain balance, especially on the rapid strides at the beginning of a race. Once up to speed, the arms work in concert with her legs to put all of her 130 pounds into each stride by aiding in her weight shift.

ACT LIKE MARLON BRANDO

Born:	**April 3, 1924**
Birthplace:	**Omaha, Nebraska, USA**
Died:	**July 1, 2004**

Widely regarded as the greatest movie actor of all time and one of the first method actors. He received eight Academy Award nominations, and won the best actor Oscar in 1954 for *On the Waterfront* and in 1972 for *The Godfather*.

Was Brando born with his incredible gift or was it taught to him—or both? Brooding, raw, honest—nobody had seen anything like him before.

WHAT IS METHOD ACTING?

Many people are aware that Brando was one of the earliest method actors, but have little idea what this actually involves. Even though Brando achieved worldwide fame in the 1950s, method acting has its roots much earlier and was introduced by a Russian actor named Constantin Stanislavski in the early twentieth century. He called it "The System," and approached the script by examining what each character wants in any given scene and the obstacles they need to overcome in order to achieve it. Actors were encouraged to perform exercises which enabled them to bring their own emotional experiences to bear upon the performance, by endowing props and other characters with personal significance that could trigger real emotions rather than the overblown theatricality that was the norm. Above all, emotional truth was dependent upon the actor focusing upon the character's wants.

c

a

73

During the 1930s, Stanislavski's teaching was developed by a theater collective called the Group Theater, which included method luminaries such as Stella Adler, Lee Strasberg, and Elia Kazan (who taught Brando there and directed him in *A Streetcar Named Desire* and *On the Waterfront*). In 1947, Kazan founded The Actor's Studio, a theatrical school and workshop in New York City, and continued to develop and teach what has now become known as the Method. Its legendary alumni included James Dean, Marilyn Monroe, Paul Newman, Robert De Niro, Dustin Hoffman, and Al Pacino.

b ☐

WHEN DID HE GET NOTICED?

When Brando played Stanley Kowalski—his first starring role—in Tennessee Williams's *A Streetcar Named Desire*, his impact was immediate. On opening night on December 3, 1947, in the words of Richard Schickel, Brando's biographer, "Our standards for performance, our expectations of what an actor should offer us in the way of psychological truth and behavioral honesty, were forever changed."

c ☒

WHY WAS HE SO SPECIAL?

For the first time an actor had given a performance that was full of brutality, conflict, and ugliness as well as beauty, passion, and animal magnetism. Before Brando, movie and theater audiences hadn't been offered anything other than performances that were well-crafted and artistically safe. According to Elia Kazan, Brando was "uncertain about himself" and "passionate, both at the same time." Brando's traumatic childhood and his neglect by his alcoholic parents must have played a major part in forging his emotional rawness. Anthony Quinn said of him, "I admire Marlon's talent, but I don't envy the pain that created it." It was what

Richard Schickel calls this "rough ambivalence," this mixture of vulnerability and strength that "articulated the postwar generation's previously inarticulate disgust with American blandness and dishonesty, its struggles to speak its truest feelings . . ."

He had an incredible ability to focus and inhabit an acting role moment to moment. Brando's presence on screen is always spontaneous and latent with possibilities because he is reacting in the present rather than planning ahead, or introducing business for effect as so many lesser actors do. The movie director Sidney Lumet observed, "When he wanted to work, his concentration was almost psychotic. . . . Everything that happened around him was grist for the mill. . . . The clearest illustration of that is that extraordinary scene in *On the Waterfront* when Eva Marie dropped her glove. And bang, not only was it not an interruption, it became the essence of the scene."

His acting teacher, Stella Adler, thought him "the most keenly aware, the most empathetic human being alive," but Schickel believed "he wasn't truly a Method actor; he was much more an observer of others than an explorer of his own depths," and fellow actor William Phipps agrees: "Yeah, he was a Method actor—Marlon Brando's method."

SKATEBOARD LIKE TONY HAWK

Born: May 12, 1968

Birthplace: San Diego, California, USA

The most famous and the most skilled skateboarder in the world, he is a giant in his sport even though he no longer officially competes. He has won numerous competitions and was the first person to stick a 900.

A poll among teenagers showed that Tony Hawk was America's best-known athlete after Michael Jordan, and his skateboarding, appearance, and endorsement income was estimated at $10 million per year when he was thirty-four years old. That's not bad for an athlete whose sport garnered little recognition until television network ESPN came up with the X Games in the mid-1990s. But Hawk was practicing tricks long before the TV execs had ever heard words like ollie, fakie, and noseflip—he started when he was six.

THE 900

Hawk's most noteworthy accomplishment on a skateboard was being the first person to stick a 900, which he did at the 1999 X Games. The 900—two-and-one-half mid-air turns—draws its name from the 360-degree rotation completed two-and-a-half times. Hawk had thirty-four failed attempts before successfully completing the trick.

c

b

He did it by working up to it, first mastering the 720 (think 360 x 2). The trick required a tall vertical ramp, known as a vert, and a great deal of speed. Just as his board reached the edge of the ramp, Hawk led a forceful body spin with his hips and shoulders. Once airborne, there's nothing to push off of to gain the torque necessary to spin. Look carefully and you'll see that Hawk's legs turn the opposite direction of the upper body. That increases the rotational inertia of his upper body; a large rotation of his legs is exactly cancelled by a small rotation of his outspread arms. Since the two rotations cancel each other, angular momentum stays constant at zero, and the law of conservation of angular momentum is satisfied.

The spin's velocity was crucial in the 900; as soon as the board left the ramp, gravity began to force it downward, creating a time limit for the 900-degree rotation of about one second.

HALF-PIPE TRICKS
Hawk's most famous trick was accomplished from a vert, but he's equally proficient at tricks using the half-pipe.

In the half-pipe, Hawk drops into a crouch while traversing the flat bottom of the U-shaped pipe. As he enters the sloped part of the ramp, Hawk straightens his legs, rising up. By raising his center of mass at the very beginning of the ramp's curve, he gains energy and increases his speed.

The extra speed that comes from pumping is a result of the equivalence of work and energy. As he moves into the bottom of the arc, centripetal force makes it harder than normal to raise himself. The net work performed in lifting is equivalent to a net energy gain. The energy gain becomes extra speed—and greater height at the top of the ramp.

THE "SIMPLE" OLLIE

The ollie is the basis for many more complicated tricks. To get that board to sail four feet in the air, Hawk starts by pushing down on the board. Starting in a crouch, he explosively straightens his legs and raises his arms. He puts greater force on the tail, causing the board to pivot counterclockwise around the rear wheels. When the tail hits the surface, the ground exerts an upward force, causing the board to rotate the opposite direction around its center of mass. With the board in the air, Hawk slides his front foot toward the nose; the friction helps drag the board even higher. Simultaneously he lifts his back foot, allowing the tail to fly upward. Hawk times this move so well it appears his feet are stuck to the deck. It allows the board to level out and Hawk uses his knees to absorb the shock upon landing.

MAKE PEOPLE LAUGH LIKE MATT GROENING

Born: **February 15, 1954**

Birthplace: **Portland, Oregon, USA**

Cartoonist best known as the creator of *The Simpsons* and *Futurama*. Both his father and one of his sons are named Homer.

Matt Groening, self-described "out-of-touch hippie" with a strong anti-authoritarian streak, goofed around at school, and is now a multi-millionaire hailed as a comedy genius who has held a mirror up to America for the last twenty years. What's the secret of his success?

a ☐ WATCH LOTS OF TV

Groening says of his childhood, "I grew up completely overwhelmed by TV, and part of the reason why I have gone into television is as a way to justify to myself all those wasted hours of watching TV as a kid. I can now look back and say, 'Oh that was research.'" He's assimilated decades of mass media bombardment, and he now makes it one of his biggest targets.

b ☒ DON'T BE LIKE EVERYONE ELSE

He has made a living out of following his interests, exploring the things that anger, worry, and freak him out, presenting absurdity, and laughing at hypocrisy. "Basically, everything I try to do is to present an alternative to what somebody else is doing," he said in reference to *Futurama*, but the remark can be applied to all his work.

"I knew that other kids were going to get serious and go on and be professionals," says Groening. "I never wanted to go to an office and carry a briefcase. I said, 'That's no fun. I want to play. I want to make up stories.'" He refused to listen to people who told him that goofing off writing cartoons would be his undoing. He started off with a photocopied cartoon called *Life in Hell* which he sold in the record store where he worked after college. The characteristic Groening overbites were present even then. Today, it is syndicated nationally and he still keeps it going, despite his other huge successes.

b

His post-college years of making ends meet shaped his worldview further as he held lots of low-paying casual jobs—"the standard stuff you do when you're trying to live by your wits and nobody's hiring," as he told Ted Anthony.

c ☐ READ THE ROZZ-TOX MANIFESTO

Written by cartoonist Gary Panter in 1980, it is an 18-point document which describes itself as "a 1980 artifact with end of the millennium resonances." Groening has said, "I read this, and was very much influenced by it, especially Item 12: 'Waiting for art talent scouts? There are no art talent scouts. Face it, no one will seek you out.' And Item 15: 'If you want better media, go make it.'"

d ☐ EXPECT TO BE A SIDESHOW

He doesn't pretend that cartoons are an art form and has said "I always think it's a mistake for cartoonists to demand cartoons be treated as art. Cartoons are cartoons." The best ones are usually not in the mainstream but, "They're the most fun thing out there. So what if you don't get respect?" But that didn't stop him from bringing his unique brand of anarchic subversion to a mass audience.

e ☐ WRITE ABOUT THE BIG STUFF

In an interview with Richard von Busack in 1986, the year before *The Simpsons* first appeared on the *Tracy Ulmann Show*, Groening said, "Most of what I write about is stuff that keeps people laying awake at night, love, work, sex, death. That covers it . . . can't go wrong with those subjects." He wasn't wrong.

TAKE PHOTOGRAPHS LIKE ANSEL ADAMS

Born:	February 20, 1902
Birthplace:	San Francisco, California, USA
Died:	April 22, 1984

Wildlife and nature photographer and pioneer, who not only produced some of the most famous and enduring images of the twentieth century, but was also a proactive conservationist who simplified and raised photography to an art form.

At the age of fourteen Adams visited Yosemite in California which inspired him for the rest of his life. He revisited the spectacular national park during every summer of his career. In 1930 he met Paul Strand, who was using a technique called "straight" photography which was highly naturalistic and sharply focused. This greatly influenced Adams. Two years later Adams got together with several other Californian realistic photographers; they formed Group f/64 (which refers to the smallest aperture marked on a standard reflex camera) and aimed to produce technically perfect prints in high realism. In fact, what Adams pioneered was not "straight" photography but his unique subjective and personal response to the natural world.

 WHAT EQUIPMENT DID HE USE?

He used a large format camera, well stopped down (this means that the aperture is small), and he often developed the prints by contact rather than by shining a light through the negatives, which made for much greater definition and clarity. He used smooth silver gelatine paper for super-fine definition and high contrast.

b ☐

WHY WAS HE A PIONEER?

He was a technical pioneer in that he invented a practical and usable system (the Zone System) to codify the techniques of exposure and development. It was very user-friendly, and didn't require graph drawing and all the other scientific methods that had previously been necessary to work out the correct aperture and exposure times. Adams's system made it much easier for the photographer to visualize what the finished print would look like, without having to resort to complicated mathematics.

c ☒

THE ZONE SYSTEM

Adams believed that photographers should have a subjective mental impression of how they want the subject to turn out on the photograph. Once they have made that vital artistic decision, their vision can be created by manipulating the different variables—camera controls, choice of film, filters, the exposure (how much light reaches the film), film development, and the printing process. All these factors influence the final result, but the whole process begins in the mind of the photographer, based on the certainty that if you can visualize an image, then you can use the technology at your disposal to create it—*if you can think it, you can print it.*

Nowadays, of course, with high-contrast developing paper, digital cameras, and photo-manipulation software, tinkering with an image to get what you want is much easier than it was in Adams's day. It is still important for a photographer to take responsibility as the artist, to have a clear subjective response to what he or she is shooting, and then make a single-minded effort to turn that image into a reality. Adams's legacy is more pertinent today than it has ever been.

BE HAPPY LIKE
THE DALAI LAMA

Born: July 6, 1935

Name at Birth: Lhamo Thondup

Birthplace: Taktser, Amdo province, Tibet

The exiled spiritual and political leader of Tibet and head of the *Dge-lugs-pa* (Yellow Hat) Buddhist school. He was awarded the Nobel Peace Prize in 1989.

Born into a peasant family in northeastern Tibet, he was recognized at the age of two (in keeping with Tibetan tradition) as the reincarnation of his predecessor the thirteenth Dalai Lama, Tenzin Gyatso. The Dalai Lamas are the manifestations of the Bodhisattva of Compassion and Dalai Lama means "Ocean of Wisdom." Tibetans refer to him as *Yeshin Norbu*, "the Wish-fulfilling Gem," or *Kundun*, "The Presence."

THE MEANING OF LIFE

The Dalai Lama has said over and over again that the sole purpose of existence is happiness. We are born to achieve happiness and it is the meaning of our lives. He has often cited plants and animals in this context. Plants, he says, do not have fixed goals or attachments; they just grow. "Animals," he says "seem to have happiness as their aim." And for humans, compassion is the force of growth.

c

b

HOW TO BE HAPPY

The Dalai Lama, like all great sages, does not claim to be anyone special (he refers to himself as a "simple monk") or to say anything new. His philosophy is simple: happiness is achieved by developing compassion for others. Happier people are more likely to show kindness toward others, while showing kindness toward other people makes people happier. However, like any art, he attests that being happier requires study and practice, and a natural talent that he says is within all of us. For this reason "all sentient beings have the seed of the Buddha within them" but "happiness is not something ready made. It comes from your own actions" and "involves an inner discipline, a gradual process of rooting out destructive mental states and replacing them with positive, constructive states of mind, such as kindness, tolerance, and forgiveness."

THE PURSUIT OF HAPPINESS THROUGH WISDOM

The Dalai Lama is an educated man, but he stresses that "those who use their minds too much are unhappier than the simple people who don't." He attributes this to the fact that they have "too much desire, hatred, and jealousy." His antidote lies in "increasing the right kind of knowledge," and he says that wisdom can only be attained by "knowledge coupled with a warm heart."

COMPASSION BRINGS CALMNESS

The Dalai Lama often makes a link between calmness and compassion. He says that compassion automatically brings happiness and calmness, and that those who are agitated can be thrown off balance even by minor disturbances. The Buddhist word *karuna* expresses the act of doing something good for another person—even an enemy—without expectations, and even without the other person being aware of your actions.

People who show *karuna* toward an enemy may not heal the enemy, but they do heal themselves by letting go of destructive emotions and calming the mind.

e ☐ DOES HE GET ANGRY?

"Oh yes, I do. Negative emotions come and go. I do not think they remain within me for long. If you let anger remain within you, it leads to ill-feeling and hatred." He stresses the need to view one's anger objectively and to see the positive side. But he is always aware that he can change and calm his mind.

f ☐ SHUNYATA AND HAPPINESS

Shunyata is awareness of the ultimate reality of everything. The Dalai Lama says that "to purify the mind it is essential to know the nature of reality, which is *shunyata*. Negative emotions arise from a misconception of reality. In order to remove suffering, you have to meditate on *shunyata*."

Once all negative emotions have been eliminated from the mind, a human becomes a Buddha.

UNDERSTAND ANIMALS LIKE JANE GOODALL

Born:	April 3, 1934
Birthplace:	London, England, UK

British ethologist (studier of animal behavior), renowned for her ground-breaking forty-year study of the chimpanzees of Gombe Stream National Park in Tanzania. She was made a Dame of the British Empire in 2003.

Jane Goodall fantasized as a young girl about understanding animals. She thought Maureen O'Hara's portrayal of Jane in a Tarzan movie was wimpish—she believed she would have done better and she was fascinated with the story of Dr. Doolittle. The childhood daydreams turned out to be more than mindless meanderings; they were early signs of a lifelong passion, a dream to which Goodall was so committed she persevered despite conventional thinking of the time.

EARLY ENCOURAGEMENT

Goodall cites an event from her childhood, when she was about age ten. While visiting a farm, she became curious about how the eggs came out of the hens. When no one gave her a satisfactory answer, she hid in the henhouse for four hours to find out. It was her first encounter with animal observation, and the first encouragement in her special interests from her mother.

"When my mother saw me rushing toward the house, she noticed my excitement," Goodall wrote. "Instead of scolding me for disappearing for so long (the family had even called the police!), she sat down and listened to me tell the wonderful story of how a hen lays an egg."

A WILLINGNESS TO DEFY CONVENTION

Goodall has a healthy sense of ignoring the rules, a trait that was crucial to her success in integrating herself with the chimpanzees at the Gombe Stream Research Center, part of the Gombe National Park in Tanzania, Africa. Despite the fact that her family had no money to send her to a university (she attended secretarial school instead), Goodall, with no scientific credentials, set out to live with primates.

She ignored contrary advice and accepted a friend's invitation to visit Kenya. While there, she brashly sought out celebrated paleontologist and anthropologist Dr. Louis Leakey. He was impressed enough to offer her a job and later recommended her as the person who should conduct the chimpanzee study she had proposed—an idea that was met with disdain by both the scientific community (due to her lack of academic training) and the government officials (who believed a woman had no chance to survive on her own in the African forest). Eventually they acquiesced, but only after Goodall's mother agreed to be her chaperone.

PATIENCE

Goodall typically started her days in Gombe before sunrise, breakfast consisting of a slice of bread and a cup of coffee. She wouldn't eat again until returning to camp in the evening. The chimpanzees were no more welcoming than the scientists; Goodall spent six months observing the primates with binoculars before she was able to get within 1,500 feet of them. All the while, Goodall contended with the other forest inhabitants—cobras and leopards among them.

Even when she accidentally stepped from behind a tree to find two chimpanzees less than twenty yards away, she simply sat down and waited.

She wrote of that first close encounter: "Very slowly I sat down, and after a few moments, the two calmly began to groom one another . . . I could almost hear them breathing . . . this was the proudest moment I had known. I had been accepted."

UNCONVENTIONAL METHODS

Continuing her pattern of disregarding custom, Goodall opted to study the chimpanzees as they lived, rather than capture and observe them in a controlled environment. Once accepted by the apes, she followed them through the forest, taking notes of her observations. Her methods allowed her to discover that chimpanzees used tools, such as sticks to encourage insects from their hiding places, putting to rest the belief that only humans had such intellect and capability. She documented emotions and familial relationships, as well as acts of kindness and brutality, for more than fifteen years.

Her patience, compassion, and persistence, coupled with a willingness to think for herself instead of accepting the norm, allowed Goodall to understand more about the primates she studied than any of her predecessors.

SAW A WOMAN IN HALF LIKE HORACE GOLDIN

Born:	December 17, 1873
Name at Birth:	Hyman Goldstein
Birthplace:	Vilna, Poland
Died:	August 21, 1939

One of the most important stage illusionists in the history of magic, whose trademark was his lightning-quick conjuring style.

In 1921, a British magician by the name of Percy Tibbles—who devised his stage name P. T. Selbit by reversing his own—performed a spectacular magic trick which had never been seen before. His female assistant lay down horizontally on a table to which she was securely strapped. Selbit covered her entire body with a wooden box, then proceeded to saw through the box and apparently right through the middle of the woman inside and through the table. When he lifted up the box again she was revealed unharmed.

However, after Selbit's sawing debut, another magician, Horace Goldin, claimed that he had invented a similar illusion twelve years earlier but he hadn't used it in his act. The most likely explanation for this is that he had a male assistant and the dynamic was not the same. His method was different, because the assistant's head and hands were visible poking out of hole in the box throughout the act, and there were no straps. After he had finished sawing, Goldin separated the box into two parts. It is this version of the sawing-a-woman-in-half trick that audiences are most familiar with today.

HOW DID GOLDIN DO IT?

The trick uses two women. When the box is brought onto the stage a woman is already hidden in one end of the box. As soon as the assistant climbs into the box, the hidden woman sticks her feet out of one end, while curling her head over her knees. The assistant brings her knees up to her chin, so that the saw passes through the box in between the two women.

A later version of this trick had the woman standing upright. This uses just one model. The box is wide enough to allow a slim model to turn sideways, while keeping her head facing forward, and her hands visible. Blades are pushed through the box in two places so that she appears to be cut into three pieces. The middle of the box is then either opened up to reveal that her midsection is missing, or the box is pulled sideways. In fact there are two factors which make the trick work. The handles are bigger than the blades, giving the illusion that the blade fills the entire box, and when the box is pulled sideways, the end is painted black, behind which the woman's midsection is hiding.

BUZZ SAW ILLUSION

Goldin is also credited with inventing the buzz saw illusion in which a woman is cut in half using a large circular saw. Like all dismemberment illusions it relies on the audience's perception of the geometry of the human body, and some clever use of mirrors.

CLEAN HOUSE LIKE LINDA COBB

Born: 1950

Birthplace: Michigan, USA

She used to run one of the largest cleaning companies in Michigan and as the Queen of Clean®, she has appeared on many TV shows in the U.S. She is a bestselling author and is in demand as a speaker and cleaning expert. She is also the great-granddaughter of baseball legend Ty Cobb.

Linda Cobb combines a positive and winning personality with expert practical knowledge to ensure that she has never been beaten by a cleaning challenge. She is also a top-notch speaker who loves to share her resourceful know-how.

GET ORGANIZED

When Linda Cobb cleans a house, the first thing she does is get organized—before she organizes. She sets a schedule so that certain chores get done on certain days, preferably at a fixed time. First she gathers supplies, which helps her avoid wasting time running downstairs to get a broom, then going down a second time to get the dustpan, returning yet again for the paper towels. That kind of inefficiency can make a five-minute cleanup take fifteen. She gets it all together—and takes it with her the first time.

GET HAPPY

The Queen of Clean makes housework a little bit fun. She might turn off the phone and turn up the stereo with a CD that makes her feel happy and energetic or pop in a book on tape. Sorting socks will never be the highlight of her week, but she'll attack it with more energy and get it done faster if the environment has her mood and energy level on an upswing.

FIND WHAT WORKS

Cobb has an arsenal of secret weapons, little known methods to deal with the worst of cleaning problems. Here are a few of the tricks she uses to make her house sparkle.

She shampoos her shirts: Hair shampoo is made to wash away body oils. Scrub a little into that dirty ring around the collar and keep an inexpensive bottle in the laundry room. It can help with other oily stains, too, and it's handy when traveling.

She uses peroxide on the couch: Hydrogen peroxide dissolves blood-stains without harming fabric. Pour a small amount on the stain and rub gently. The technique works on clothing as well as furniture. Cornstarch works on blood, too. Rinse the stain in cold water, then rub in moistened cornstarch. Place the item in the sun.

She has a big hair day: Hairspray can do a lot more than keep a bouffant intact during a Houston summer. Not only will it take magic marker ink off the wall, it kills flies too. Ah, you say, but then there's hairspray on the wall. No problem. That comes off easily by spraying it with a solution of one part liquid fabric softener and two parts water. Spray and wipe—it also does a nice job of shining the vanity.

She glues the carpet: A burn mark in the carpet doesn't mean you have to pull the whole thing up and start over. Cut out the burned fibers, squeeze a little glue onto the spot, and fill it with matching fibers trimmed from a remnant.

She has the house vinaigrette: White vinegar does some nifty things, in addition to cleaning the innards of your coffee maker. A bowl of it set on the counter will clear smoke odor from the room, and when a half-cup follows an equal amount of baking soda down the drain it's sure to keep things flowing if you let it sit for thirty minutes before flushing with cool water. Vinegar and lemon juice are both good remedies for hard water spots, too.

DJ LIKE PAUL VAN DYK

Born: December 16, 1971

Birthplace: Eisenhüttenstadt, Germany

One of the world's leading trance artists, DJ, and remixers, whose 2000 album, *Out There and Back*, turned him into a superstar on the music scene.

From early Berlin techno and house to progressive trance, the pedigree of producer/DJ Paul Van Dyk was plain to see when he began mixing in the early 1990s. His DJ and re-mixing skills have made him rich and have turned him into a hunky globetrotting club legend. Here are some of the basics that you need to master if you fancy yourself with a pair of decks.

HOW TO CHOOSE YOUR EQUIPMENT

If you're going to use vinyl, you'll need two decks (direct-drive, not cheaper belt-driven ones which are trash), two slip mats, two needles, a mixer, a pair of headphones, and an amp (so you can hear what you're mixing) against the PA system. You need a deck with lots of speed control—not just 33 or 45 rpm—and you need to be able to crank it up or down by eight to ten points either way when you're mixing.

If you're on a budget, spend as much as you can afford on the decks and then purchase the rest of the equipment with what you have left. You can use a cheap mixer with good decks, but not the other way round, plus it's easier to upgrade your other stuff than your decks. We won't waste time here telling you how to use your equipment—read the instructions. What you need to know is why and how to mix.

WHAT'S THE POINT OF DJ'ING?

The main aim of a DJ is to run an event that keeps people dancing, controls their heartbeats, and runs one track into another seamlessly so no one notices the change. Once you match the beats per minute (bpm) of the clubber's heartbeat to the bass of the song, something special happens. You want to reach a bpm where everyone feels good and is enjoying themselves without giving them an embolism. Basically, you want to start slower and build up so that you work the room to build a great energy. So maybe you start off with some warm-up tunes around 128 bpm, then crank it up to 135 and when the place is really smoking, you're on at least 140—but you don't want to go too high, or everyone will flake out before the evening is finished.

WHAT'S THE POINT OF MIXING?

Apart from choosing lots of solid tunes that blow everyone away, the number-one aim of mixing is to end one song and begin another one seamlessly. So what you need to do is have one deck running while you set up the other deck. Start the second deck running from the beginning until you hear the first beat (this is on your head-phones—only you can hear this). When you hear the first beat, put your finger on the record and wind it back to the beginning of the beat, then stop the deck (press stop). Now you've got the second tune ready to go on a beat. Listen to the beats of the first deck and, still holding the record on the second deck with your finger, press start—if you've got good slip mats and a decent direct drive deck, the turntable should start going underneath while the record stays still. Then when you're ready to let rip, release finger pressure and let the second deck play the tune (it's similar to hitting the skill feature on a gaming machine, only it's aural not visual). The two tunes should blend seamlessly so that your crowd stays in the groove. If you've screwed it up, you'll need to use your finger again to speed up (nudge) or slow down the second deck until the two decks are in sync. Don't leave your bedroom until it's in your bones.

BE A LEADER LIKE ALEXANDER THE GREAT

Born:	**356 B.C.**
Birthplace:	**Pella, Macedonia**
Died:	**June 13, 323 B.C.**

King of Macedonia from 336-323 B.C., legendary fighter, leader, and diplomat.

Alexander the Great is arguably the greatest leader who has ever lived. By his untimely death at the age of thirty-three, he had conquered and united the whole of the known world, and his empire covered one million square miles from India to Greece.

EARLY YEARS

His parents provided the very best education during his childhood. His first tutor, Leonidas, was a harsh taskmaster who taught Alexander the virtue of Spartan living and the ability to suffer pain, hunger, thirst, and great hardship that was vital on his campaigns. His next teacher, Lysimachus, taught him to play the lyre and to appreciate the arts. His third teacher was Aristotle, with whom he learned philosophy, ethics, politics, and healing. Without this extraordinary education, and his own passion for it (he knew Homer's *Iliad* by heart, slept with it under his pillow, and used it as a blueprint for his battle campaigns), his future conquests would have been impossible.

c

b ☐

COURAGE

Alexander's courage was one of the biggest inspirations he gave to his men. He always led his army into battle from the front and often placed himself in extreme danger. He was wounded many times, but always refused medical treatment until his men had received it first.

c ☒

ORGANIZATIONAL SKILLS

His courage would have counted for nothing without his ability to strategically manage his army with unprecedented skill. He had tactical flexibility and he was very willing to delegate authority, meaning that his army was more flexible, where other armies were hampered by being centrally controlled. He ate and slept with his men and rewarded them richly after every victory, giving each of his leaders a large sum of money to distribute.

d ☐

TRUST

He trusted others and inspired them to excel for him. He was a great believer in teamwork. He even trusted a nine-year-old shepherd boy to lead an army over the Uxion mountains in Persia. Like all great leaders, he gave those in his charge the opportunity to shine.

e ☐

SELF-BELIEF

Every leader needs this quality, but Alexander firmly believed he was invincible (the Oracle had told him so) and godlike. His family was reputed to be descended from the epic hero Hercules. He was also inspired by the god Dionysus, by the hero Achilles (whose tomb he visited to take the great warrior's shield for his own), and by Homer who often appeared to him in his dreams. It is hard to believe that Alexander ever doubted himself.

☐ RUTHLESSNESS

When his father, Philip of Macedon, died there was some dispute as to whether Alexander or his infant half brother should succeed him. Alexander settled the matter by killing the baby and all those who supported the baby's claim to the throne.

☐ SIMPLE SOLUTIONS

Alexander's character is best represented by his approach to solving the Gordian Knot, which legend held would only be untied by a man who would conquer the known world. Alexander slashed it with his sword and then unpicked the pieces, upon which the Egyptians hailed him as their immortal pharaoh and Alexander built his city of Alexandria.

☐ RESPECT FOR OTHER CULTURES

Alexander fell out with his great mentor Aristotle, because the latter felt that foreigners were barbarians, whereas Alexander always respected the cultures of those he conquered and took wives from three different countries to forge strategic alliances. He was quick to crush revolt—he slaughtered all the inhabitants of unruly Thebes as an example to the rest of Greece—but he didn't capture and enslave, or try to impose his own religion and culture on others; instead he melded Greek and local culture in a positive way. For this quality Fred Smith, founder and CEO of Federal Express, described Alexander as "the first truly global thinker."

PITCH A CURVEBALL LIKE SANDY KOUFAX

Born: December 30, 1935

Birthplace: Brooklyn, New York, USA

Major League Baseball pitcher and Hall of Famer. He is widely regarded as the most dominant pitcher in the history of the game. He won 25 or more games three times, won five straight ERA titles, and in 1965 he had 382 strikeouts as well as a perfect game.

When Los Angeles Dodgers left-handed pitcher Sandy Koufax learned to control his blistering speed he dominated the game for the next five years, but like most pitching legends he really knew how to mix things up with his awesome curve.

a ☐ WHAT IS A CURVEBALL?

A curveball is a pitch with topspin that seems to be heading straight for home plate, but actually moves down and to the right or left by as much as sixteen inches. It's one of the hardest pitches to hit, and the sign of a good curveball is when it forces the batter to jump out of its way. A curveball is a slower pitch, and in general the slower it is the more spin can be applied to the ball.

b ☐ A WORD OF WARNING

First off, a pitcher should only start throwing curveballs when he or she is physically mature. Many coaches recommend waiting until age sixteen, because the throw can cause serious damage to the shoulder, elbow, and wrist of someone who is physically immature. There are countless stories of eleven-year-olds who pitch a curve without pain, only to find that three years later they have done permanent damage and can't throw without feeling pain. In Little League it's not worth it anyway, because the ball doesn't travel far enough to permit a big break. Also, remember that the fastball is the staple of most pitchers, and the curve should only be used about five percent of the time.

☒ THROW A CURVEBALL

Hold the ball with your thumb on the bottom of the ball and your middle and index fingers on top, perpendicular to the seam at its widest point. Keep the pinkie and ring finger bent in to the palm.

Grip the ball firmly and squeeze with the middle finger and thumb. Don't rest the ball in the palm and keep the index finger relaxed.

Use the same pitching action as you would for any pitch, so as not to give away the fact that you are throwing a curve. But after you have drawn back your arm, bend the wrist back.

At the end of the pitch, roll the wrist downwards and away to the side (to the right for a right-hander, left for a left-hander). This gives the ball topspin.

Follow through after releasing the ball by bending the wrist so that the back of the pitching hand is facing the batter.

☐ THE MAGNUS FORCE

The ball curves in the direction of the spin because as it travels through the air it meets more resistance at the top of the ball than the bottom. This is because at the bottom the ball spins with the airflow and the air moves faster around it. This faster moving air creates lower pressure than the slower moving air at the top of the ball and this makes the ball fall downwards. It is the same principal that gives an airplane lift and enables David Beckham to bend his free kicks (*see page 132*). It is named for physicist Gustav Magnus, who discovered this principle in 1852 after observing spinning objects moving through liquids.

A STITCH IN TIME

There are 108 red stitches on a baseball and they also have a big effect on how the ball moves through the air. They increase the amount of friction the ball experiences as it travels the sixty feet and six inches from pitcher to batter.

WHEELCHAIR RACE LIKE JEAN DRISCOLL

Born:	November 18, 1966
Birthplace:	Milwaukee, Wisconsin, USA

Winner of the Boston Marathon eight times in the wheelchair division (a record of wins unparalleled over all of the divisions). Winner of two Olympic silver medals and twelve Paralympic medals.

Jean Driscoll was born with spina bifida, a congenital birth defect that affects the spinal column. Despite this, she has had an unprecedented sporting career. She retired in 2000, and continues to be an inspirational speaker, trainer, and motivator who was voted number 25 in the Top 100 Female Athletes of the Twentieth Century by _Sports Illustrated for Women_.

 STRENGTH TRAINING

Four times a week Jean spent ninety minutes in the gym doing resistance training and lifting weights. During the winter she used a specially designed off-road wheelchair in the snow to build her endurance. The Boston Marathon course is famous for its hills, but living in flat Illinois, Jean had to find a substitute to prepare; so she trained in a headwind to increase the drag. In an interview she described her gruelling wind training: "The winds here [Illinois] are unforgiving . . . you stop pushing, you slow down. In some cases you almost feel like it's going to push you backwards." She also powered up and down the entry ramps at the Assembly Hall at Illinois University, often dragging a friend behind her for an added challenge.

AEROBIC TRAINING

Jean used an Upper Body Ergometer (UBE) which is like pedaling a bike with your hands. She also had special equipment called "rollers" designed for her by her trainer and mechanical engineering students at the University of Illinois. This enabled her to simulate the wheel pushing action while being hooked up to a computer which could interact with the hardware to simulate hills and headwinds. She combined this with video footage of a race to get as close as possible to the real thing.

Footballers, sprinters, and other elite sportspeople are routinely video-taped while they train in order to analyze their technique. Jean's roller sessions were recorded to allow her and her coach to maximize her efficiency and ensure that she was achieving the optimum aerodynamic shape.

She also pounded out hundreds of miles a month on the road, doing a range of distances—short sprints, medium, and long distance work. When a group of wheelers train together they can practice a technique shared by cyclists, distance runners, and migrating birds, called "drafting." This involves taking it in turns to lead the pack while the others fall in behind and benefit from the slipstream.

MENTAL PREPARATION

In common with many sportspeople, Jean was a great visualizer. She pictured each race in great detail. This allowed her to reinforce in her mind how she would cope with potential problems such as a flat tire as well as mapping tactics and convincing herself that she would cross the finish-line first.

Today in her role as motivator and professional speaker she says, "You've got to be willing to take risks. Dream big, set big goals, and then work hard to make your dreams happen."

CLIMB A MOUNTAIN LIKE SIR EDMUND HILLARY

Born: July 20, 1919

Birthplace: Auckland, New Zealand

Mountain climber and Antarctic explorer; with Sherpa Tenzing Norgay, the first person to reach the summit of Mt. Everest.

As a boy Edmund Hillary took long walks and daydreamed of adventure. Not long after, Hillary again had his head in the clouds—literally. With Sherpa Tenzing Norgay, Hillary became the first person to reach the top of the world—the summit of Mt. Everest, 29,035 feet above sea level.

THE RIGHT TEAM

Hillary was part of a 1953 expedition that was organized by Colonel John Hunt. Hunt hand-picked the team members, all young men with extensive mountaineering experience who were in excellent shape.

Hillary and Norgay were the second assault team to attempt the summit. Three days before the famous climb, another pair ascended to the mountain's South Summit, but weather and problems with their oxygen supplies prevented them from going further. All mountaineers learn from those who have climbed before them, and Hillary benefitted greatly from details the two reported upon their return.

MAKING THE MOST OF A BREAK

When Hillary and Norgay ascended the last thousand feet to the summit on the morning of May 29, the only unknown part of the trek stretched from the South Summit to the top of the mountain. The greatest geographic challenge was a great rock step, impossible to climb at an altitude of nearly 29,000 feet. But Hillary had the experience to recognize even an unusual means of ascent. To his right he spied an ice cornice clinging to the rock, hanging over the Kangshung Face. Gravity had broken the ice away from the rock, leaving a narrow crack. Hillary slithered into the narrow fissure, and, driving his crampons into the ice behind him, managed to slither up forty feet to the top of the rock step.

MENTAL MATH

The most dangerous part of the Everest climb was lack of oxygen. Above 25,000 feet, the atmosphere has only about one-third of the oxygen that is available at sea level. Consequently, climbers can experience hallucinations, brain swelling, nausea, lack of coordination, confusion, and rapid exhaustion. One of the talents that allowed Hillary to succeed where so many others had failed was his ability to mentally calculate how many hours of oxygen were available in his canister. Typically sleeping on one liter of oxygen per hour for four hours, Hillary knew with precision how far he could go. As a result, he and Norgay spent just fifteen minutes at the top.

d ☐

CUTTING STEPS

At high altitudes, mountains are nothing but ice, snow, and boulders.
Near the top of Mt. Everest, the temperature never gets warmer than
-2 degrees Fahrenheit (-19° C). Hillary was particularly adept at cut-
ting steps into the ice with his ax. He had such a knack for it that
he often recut Norgay's steps to make them safer and make traversing
them easier.

e ☐

KEEPING HEALTHY

The expedition's physician was an expert on the physiological effects
of high altitude climbing. Hillary took careful note of the doctor's
warnings, which allowed him to maintain his strength on the climb.
Appetite evaporates at extreme altitude, but Hillary forced himself to
maintain his energy by drinking weak tea loaded with sugar. He was
also keenly aware of the risk of dehydration and consumed great
quantities of water daily.

f ☒

PSYCHOLOGICAL STRENGTH

Careful planning, execution, teamwork, and a bit of luck got Edmund
Hillary to the top of the world, but without extraordinary confidence and
will, the physical elements wouldn't have gotten him to the summit. As
Hillary once said, "It is not the mountain we conquer, it is ourselves. If
you can overcome your fear, you are frequently able to extend yourself
far beyond what you normally regard as your ability."

HAVE A GREAT MEMORY LIKE ANDI BELL

Born: **December 17, 1967**

Birthplace: **Hertfordshire, UK**

He has been World Memory Champion three times and holds the world speed record for memorizing a single pack of cards in 32.9 seconds.

Andi Bell has a remarkable memory and yet he claims that anyone can perform the incredible feats of memory which have made him three-time World Memory Champion and an awe-inspiring "mentathlete."

In June 2003, he successfully memorized a hundred decks of playing cards in five hours, and then when he was asked questions like "What is the fifteenth card in the seventy-eighth pack?" he answered eighty-nine percent of questions correctly. He was able to hold a sequence of 5,200 cards in his mind—an astonishing feat, made possible by what he calls his "location technique" which he says, once learned, "takes everything beyond what you can do naturally."

a

HOW DOES IT WORK?

Bell explains the location technique: "You have got to think of the things you want to remember against a mental backdrop of places that you know." He doesn't remember cards as such—he converts each one into an animal or a colorful object. For example, the queen of hearts may become a jam tart, the two of diamonds a pair of balloons, and the four of spades a banana. To memorize a sequence he places these items in groups of three along the route of a mental journey around the streets of London. Before a memory challenge, he picks a route in London and he actually walks along it, committing it to memory and choosing places where he can dump his visual memories—doorways, bus stops, landmarks, etc. Then, when he wants to recall them, he mentally returns to a particular part of the route, "hopefully seeing the images still there, and turn[ing] them back into the cards."

The associations he has created for each card are visually rich and often absurd, since the more outlandish an image, the easier it is to recall.

DID HE INVENT IT?

Andi Bell actually uses a method that is 2,500 years old and was written about by a Greek scholar, Simonides, and became known as the "Method of Loci." In 477 B.C., he was dining in a banquet hall with many other assembled guests when the roof collapsed, killing many. Simonides escaped, and was able to name all the victims by recalling where they had been sitting during the meal.

WHY DOES IT WORK?

When a person memorizes something, he or she creates a link or links between various brain cells, of which we all have over a hundred billion. Something that is memorized weakly will only correspond to one neural connection, whereas a strong memory may have many. The location technique is effective because a familiar location has already created thousands of neural connections, involving the five senses. Adding new items into that context helps to reinforce the memory, because the connections are already well established; anything else that becomes associated with them is more likely to be recalled.

TRACK ANIMALS LIKE TOM BROWN, JR.

Born: **January 29, 1950**

Birthplace: **Toms River, New Jersey, USA**

America's leading outdoorsman and one of the most skilled and accomplished trackers in the world. He trains the general public as well as Navy SEALS and forest rangers.

Tom Brown, Jr. learned his skills as a child and teenager from an eighty-year-old Apache elder named Stalking Wolf, the grandfather of a school friend, who passed on his deep knowledge of tracking, awareness, and wilderness survival. Brown and his wife Debra run the world's largest tracking, nature, and wilderness survival school in the New Jersey Pine Barrens, and he is frequently asked by the police and FBI to help track down missing persons, fugitives, and lost hikers.

Every animal leaves tracks which reveal a lot of information: "Tracks are like miniature landscapes. If you lift your arm, your body shifts to compensate. Those compensations leave 'pressure releases' in your tracks," says Brown. "With experience, you can read if an animal has stopped, if it's anxious, if it's tired, even if it has a full belly." He can tell the breed of animal, sex, age, state of health, its motivation, and mental state. "Every pock, hill, dome, etc. is the track of something. A dent in the forest floor may be the track of a fallen branch."

SIGNS

There is a range of signs—large, medium, and small. Large-scale signs call for observing the landscape to find areas which favor herbivores, which in turn attract carnivores. If a tracker locates signs of voles, a common food source for many predators, it is a safe bet that there will be rabbits and other animals. Large signs also include animal sleeping and eating areas.

Medium-scale signs include branches and other objects which an animal has brushed against, leaving fur, hair, feathers, bite marks, chewing and scratching marks, and, of course, scat (animal droppings). Talking about vole scat, Brown says, "Vole scat's neat. If it's bright green, it's fresh. Brown-green, it's a day old. Brown, two days old. Black, it's a week old."

Small-scale signs include "compressions" and their detection requires a technique called "sideheading" which involves putting your head down along the ground. You use your bottom eye to look along the line of the tracks in the direction of the sun to spot compressions. The grit or dust that has been squashed into the track shows up differently from the surroundings.

WALKING PATTERNS

There are four kinds of walkers—diagonal, bounders, pacers, and gallopers. Diagonal walkers (deer, dogs, cats, foxes) move diagonally opposite feet at the same time—the right front foot moves with the left back foot, and the left front foot moves with the right back foot. Bounders (the weasel family, except skunks and badgers) move forward with the front feet, then the back feet follow just behind them. Pacers (badgers, skunks, opossum, porcupines, raccoons, bears) move both feet on one side of the body at the same time. Gallopers (rabbits, hares, rodents, except porcupine and groundhog) propel themselves with the back feet, landing on their front feet, then the back feet land just in front of the front feet and push off again.

Finding the tracks is just the beginning. Brown can read the information contained within them, by reading subtle details in and around the track—flats, depressions, rolls, cliffs, overhangs, slopes, gouges—a catalogue of details which Brown says numbers over four thousand.

SPEED

When animals vary their speed or accelerate, it shows in their tracks. For example, a diagonal walker such as a deer will speed up into a bounding pattern and faster still into a gallop. Pacers also change their pattern as they speed up to a diagonal walk, bound then gallop, whereas bounders remain the same, regardless of speed. These differences from the normal gait reveal an animal's motivation. For example, a skunk moving diagonally is in a hurry. Stalking animals slow down and many leave tracks resembling those of a diagonal walker.

WEIGHT

The animal's weight can be determined by looking at how deep the track is and recognizing how much weight displaces that amount of earth, allowing for other factors such as the weather and corresponding hardness of the ground.

e ☐ SEX

Male tracks are not necessarily the biggest; it is the placement of the rear track which indicates sex. In a diagonal walker, such as a deer, if the rear track lies to the outside of the front track, the animal is female; if the rear foot is inside, it's a male. Also males tend to walk on the outside edge of their hind feet, to accommodate their external sex organs.

WRITE A SPEECH LIKE MICHAEL GERSON

Born: 1965

Birthplace: New Jersey, USA

He was head speechwriter and policy adviser to President George W. Bush during his first term and is currently Assistant to the President for Policy and Strategic Planning.

Michael Gerson has been widely acknowledged to be as important and influential a figure in politics as Peggy Noonan was to Ronald Reagan or Theodore Sorenson was to John F. Kennedy. Bush's nickname for him is "The Scribe."

a ☐ POLICY CONSULTATION

Before writing a major speech, Gerson has a meeting with Bush and he records their conversation on a handheld tape recorder as the President discusses his thoughts. Senator Dan Coats (Gerson was once his policy director) has remarked on his "uncanny ability . . . to sit and talk and think aloud with you. And translate your thoughts and conclusions and recommendations into a document that seems to express it even better than you expressed it."

b ☐ OUTLINE AND DRAFTS

Bush first asks to see an outline. Only then does Gerson begin work on the first of many drafts. It is not unusual for a Bush speech to go through fifteen drafts before it is complete. This is a vital part of any writing process, but according to Gerson, the process is highly collaborative. He has a team of six writers, researchers, and fact-checkers, as well as the many White House members who see the drafts: "The complicating factor of my daily life is the staffing process, because we write beautiful things and then it goes to every senior member of the White House, and they all get a chance to comment and change things, and sometimes we get good speeches out of that process."

WHAT IS HIS TRADEMARK?

The quality which sets Gerson apart from other speech writers is the religious language and Biblical references which are peppered throughout Bush's speeches. Gerson is an evangelical Christian and a former student of theology who shares Bush's trademark "compassionate conservatism." Some critics have referred to a hidden code, which presses all the right buttons with the conservatives, but Gerson denies this: "I try to explain [to reporters] that they're not code words; they're literary references understood by millions of Americans. They're not code words; they're our culture." He believes that in political discourse, "[religious] images are given a lesser meaning, but they have an added literary resonance precisely because they have a deeper meaning." His ultimate aim, he says, is "to employ religious language in a way that unites people."

He is a man steeped in literature, who is, in the words of Bush's long time adviser Karen P. Hughes, able to "challenge the president . . . to more poetic heights" without losing his characteristic Texan plain-spokenness which Hughes calls "eloquent simplicity."

d ☐

RESEARCH

Gerson is a consummate researcher. Before he penned Bush's historic first term inaugural speech he read every single previous inaugural address.

e ☐

WHERE DOES HE WRITE?

He has a prestigious West Wing office, but he can often be found in the local coffee shop, chewed pencil in hand, writing to the sound of espresso machines. He describes his high-pressure job as "a tremendous roller coaster. Before a speech, you feel like the most important person in the world, and after a speech you're just a writer and really don't matter very much."

c

TASTE WINE LIKE ROBERT PARKER

Born: July 23, 1947

Birthplace: Baltimore, Maryland, USA

Straight-talking publisher of *The Wine Advocate*, he is the most influential wine critic in the world today. In 1999, he became one of the few foreigners to be awarded France's *Légion d'Honneur*.

Robert Parker goes through five steps to taste a wine; each offers a different sensory experience. The combination helps him answer the simplest, yet most important question: Do I like it?

a ☒ COLOR

Parker first holds the glass, preferably in front of a white surface, to look at the color. As white wine ages, it gains color, but red wine loses some of its brilliance. White wines start out a pale yellow-green, working through shades of gold before turning brown. The oldest reds are brown as well, but they get there from the opposite end of the spectrum, starting life quite purple and progressing through shades of red.

b ☐ SWIRL

When Parker swirls his wine around in his glass, he isn't playing with his food. In uppity sommelier language, he's releasing the esters, ethers, and aldehydes, yielding the wine's bouquet. In other words, he's mixing air into the wine to open up its smell. He looks at the wine trickling down the glass. If those trickles—or legs, as they're known—

are noticeable, the wine is likely to be full-bodied. If the legs are thin or nonexistent, it may indicate that the wine has a thin taste.

SMELL

Just like the rest of us, Parker's mother probably taught him not to put his nose in the glass, but that bit of etiquette doesn't apply to wineglasses. The whole point of that bowl-shaped glass is to collect the scent for easier sniffing. Parker—like the rest of us—can differentiate more than two thousand scents but only four tastes: sweet, sour, bitter, and salt.

After he's swirled, Parker smells the wine three times—that third sniff holds the most information. Here he finds the bouquet—the aroma—sometimes called the "nose."

It might smell like citrus. Or leather. Or wood. Or apricot.

Parker smells for warning signs. If he smells vinegar, he knows the wine has too much acetic acid. If he gets a whiff of sherry, he knows it's begun to oxidize. If it has a musty, dank, cork smell, Parker knows the wine has absorbed the taste of a defective cork. And if it smells like sulfur, he recognizes that as a sign that the wine has too much sulfur dioxide, which is used in the winemaking process.

TASTE

Parker doesn't take a gulp and throw it down his throat. Taste buds are all over the tongue—including the side, the tip, underneath, and all the way back to the throat. The more taste buds awash in wine, the more taste there is to experience. The tip of his tongue will identify sweetness, which comes from residual sugar after fermentation, and he'll taste it immediately. The fruitiness will hit the middle of the tongue and the acidity will be noticeable on the sides of the tongue and back of the throat. Tannin will also stimulate the middle of the tongue, and if a wine hasn't been aged adequately, the tannin can dry out the palate.

Parker is especially mindful of the aftertaste, or finish. A high quality wine will have a pleasant, lengthy finish, sometimes lasting up to three minutes.

e ☐ SAVOR

Once Parker's looked at the color, swirled to aerate, smelled and tasted, he takes a minute to let it all sink in. Was it full-bodied or light? Sweet, fruity, or bitter? He'll imagine what kind of food it would complement.

f ☒ STEM

You'll never see Parker hold his wineglass by anything but the stem. There's a reason wine is served in stemware—heat from the hand changes the temperature of the wine, which can affect the flavor. Holding the stem prevents that.

BEND IT LIKE BECKHAM

Born: May 2, 1975

Birthplace: Leytonstone, London, UK

Leading English soccer player, currently a midfielder for Real Madrid and England Captain. He is one of the best crossers and free-kickers in the world. While at Manchester United, his team won the Premier League six times and the F.A. Cup twice.

When making a free-kick, David Beckham draws upon years of practice (and some very sophisticated physics) to make the ball bend in mid-air and then drop abruptly into the goal.

TOTALLY LOGO

Becks (as fans know him) is probably the most skilled free-kicker in the world, and his free-kicks are certainly the best known in the game. In March 2004, he even unveiled his own personalized Adidas logo which was inspired by his kicks. "The image of me taking a free-kick is world renowned and instantly recognizable," says Beckham. Eric Vellozzi, the Adidas designer who developed the logo goes even further: "A David Beckham free-kick is one of the most recognizable images in world sport, even before he kicks the ball, due to the angle of his body upon impact. Couple that with the significant curve that this action puts on the flight path of the ball and you have something truly original."

b ☐

NATURAL SCIENTIST

Scientists at the Universities of Sheffield in the UK and Yamagata in Japan have scrutinized his deviating shots using wind tunnels, high-speed camera analysis, and the computer-modelling wizardry of Fluent, Inc. to try to better understand this scientific genius in a number twenty-three shirt. They paid special attention to one of his most famous free-kick goals of all time—against Greece in the 2002 World Cup qualifiers.

c ☐

NAIL BITER

England was trailing 2-1 deep into injury time and it looked as if they were going to be forced into an arduous play-off against the Ukraine. Beckham came to the rescue with a perfectly executed free-kick in the ninety-third minute which ensured England's qualification for Japan and Korea. It was an amazing climax to an otherwise unsteady performance from England.

d ☒

HOW DID HE KICK IT?

On that occasion, he booted the ball about three inches to the right of center with the instep of his right foot. The ball then accelerated rapidly to eighty miles per hour, while rotating counter-clockwise at about eight revolutions per second. It rose high in the air, started swerving to the left, and looked as though it would soar over the crossbar. At the last moment it slowed to forty miles per hour, curved sharply to the left, and swooped into the top left corner of the goal.

Two aspects of this awesome kick demand an explanation—why did the ball curve, and why did it decelerate and lose height so suddenly?

☐ THE MAGNUS FORCE, AGAIN

When a spinning ball travels through the air, it curves in the direction
of the spin, because airflow around one side of the ball is hampered
by the spin, and the other side is accelerated, causing lower pressure
on that side of the ball, so the ball is pushed towards this low-pres-
sure side. This is known as the Magnus force—the same principle that
gives an airplane lift (air takes longer to flow under the wing than
over it).

The ball loses height and decelerates rapidly because of another area
of Becks's expertise—drag (and we're not just talking about sarongs
and Alice bands). Drag is the resistance that the ball meets from
the air flowing against it. Scientists have discovered that the drag
changes dramatically at around twenty miles per hour. It is turbulent
at the high speed achieved at the beginning of the kick, but when
the ball reaches the lower speed, the drag becomes "laminar," which
means that it moves over the ball in layers, increasing by as much as
a hundred-and-fifty percent in a split second. It is this that makes the
ball drop out of the air so sharply.

☒ ACUTE ANKLE

It has also been observed that he can hinge his right ankle in such a
way that he can wrap his instep around the ball. He also twists his
body away while aiming his left shoulder at the goal, and he posi-
tions his left foot at an extreme angle from the perpendicular, which
places enormous stresses on his left ankle. It is remarkable that Becks
knows exactly how much speed and spin to apply to harness these
unique physical forces.

MAKE AN OMELETTE LIKE JULIA CHILD

Born: August 15, 1912

Name at Birth: Julia McWilliams

Birthplace: Pasadena, California, USA

Died: August 12, 2004

The first American celebrity chef, winner of Peabody and Emmy awards, bestselling author of numerous books, and recipient of the *Légion d'Honneur* in 2000.

Julia Child was always interested in cooking simply. When an omelette is cooked correctly it should be a quick and easy meal taking less than half a minute. According to Child, "A good French omelette is a smooth, gently swelling, golden oval that is tender and creamy inside."

In her book, *Mastering the Art of French Cooking,* she describes how to make *L'omelette Brouilée* (scrambled omelette), and *L'omelette Roulée* (rolled omelette), both of which are shown below. But before cooking begins there are several important provisos:

a

a ☒ THE PAN

The pan must be the correct size (seven inches bottom diameter for a three-egg omelette), so that the depth of the egg in the pan is not over 1/4 inch. The pan should have a long handle and straight sloping sides. It must also be non-stick to allow the egg to slide around.

b ☐ BEATING THE EGGS

Julia advises that a single omelette should contain two or three large eggs and no more if it is to be tender and creamy. She recommends adding salt and pepper to the eggs before whisking with a large fork up to forty strokes (no more than thirty seconds), just enough to blend the whites and the yolks.

c ☐ HEATING THE BUTTER

She places a tablespoon of butter in the pan over a high heat. Then she tilts the pan so that when the butter melts it coats the bottom and sides. She adds the egg mixture when she can see "that the foam has almost subsided in the pan and the butter is on the point of coloring."

L'omelette Brouilée: As soon as the egg has been added to the pan she slides the pan back and forth over the heat and uses the back of a fork to spread the mixture evenly. Within seconds the eggs "become a light, broken custard" (this would be the point to add filling if required). Then she tilts the pan away from her at 45 degrees and uses the fork to gather the omelette at the far edge of the pan. Julia then raps the pan handle sharply a few times to loosen the omelette and to help the far edge to flip back on itself. She then picks up the pan with an under-arm grip and tips the omelette onto a warm plate. The center of the omelette should still be "soft and creamy."

L'omelette Roulée: This method involves adding the eggs to the pan, leaving them for a few seconds, then picking up the pan with two hands and jerking it towards her "at an even, 20-degree angle over the heat, one jerk per second." Within seconds the egg thickens and detaches from the bottom of the pan (this would be the point to add filling if required). Then she tips the pan up further so that the jerking movement makes the egg mixture roll over on itself, until she is left with a neat rolled package at the far side of the pan.

In both methods the omelette should take less than thirty seconds.

INVENT LIKE THOMAS EDISON

Born: February 11, 1847

Birthplace: Milan, Ohio, USA

Died: October 18, 1931

One of the most significant and prolific inventors the world has ever known. His most famous invention was to perfect the lightbulb and he played a crucial role in introducing the age of electricity.

Inspired by curiosity and driven by competitive spirit and ego, Thomas Edison was awarded 1,093 patents, the most ever granted an individual. Beyond a resourceful mind and obsession with work, he was also a sharp businessman and marketer. The combination gave him financial success as well as scientific triumph. At his peak, Edison employed more than 2,000 people.

EARLY ACUMEN

At twelve years of age, Edison had a job on a commuter train that ran in Michigan between Port Huron and Detroit. He sold candy, newspapers, and the like to passengers, but also persuaded his employer to allow him to set up a small laboratory in a freight car so he could continue his experiments. During the long layover in Detroit, he frequented the public library to study on his own. He also persuaded a station operator to teach him to use the telegraph.

The Civil War was on and Edison realized passengers wouldn't know about the Battle of Shiloh in that day's paper. He persuaded the *Detroit Free Press* to supply him with extra copies, then telegraphed ahead that the story would be available when the train passed through. He sold all the papers, increasing the price at each stop.

FROM TELEGRAPH TO PHONOGRAPH

Edison's break came when he was able to repair an archaic telegraph system used by his employer when he was sixteen; the company reported gold prices to Wall Street, and Edison's quick repair job got him an offer from Western Union to work full time as an inventor. Ultimately, his business sense and work habits allowed him to go out on his own, building a huge, expensive laboratory.

DRIVE

Edison worked—a lot. He saw little of his first wife and lavished expensive gifts upon his second to make up for the little time he spent at home. He was known for working 112 hours per week, taking brief naps throughout the day but sleeping only four hours per night.

THE WIZARD

Part of Edison's genius was his public relations skills. Edison realized that for an invention to be commercially viable, he needed financial backing and demand in the market. With each new invention, Edison staged a creative public display of his work—and made sure to invite reporters. His introductions include recreating experiments that showed off the product's promise and usually gained extensive newspaper coverage.

ATTITUDE

"Success is ninety-nine percent perspiration and one percent inspiration," Edison said. It reflected his approach to inventions—he never gave up when he believed something could work. After 10,000 unsuccessful tries to find a filament that would work for his improvements to the electric lightbulb, he didn't consider the effort a failure. Instead, he characterized the experience by saying it was a success because he now knew 10,000 things that wouldn't work.

 A MIND AT 78 RPM

Edison's mind was always on overdrive; he reportedly once declined to exercise, saying his body was merely something he used to carry his brain around in. So active were his gray cells that he often lost track of the daily minutiae—the time, where he was, even his name. An ear injury caused him to lose much of his hearing when he was twelve, but he considered that a benefit. Rather than being distracted by chit-chat at social functions, he was free to let his mind work— usually on the details of his next invention.

PHOTO CREDITS